OVER 300 NUTRITIOUS RECIPES FOR HURRY-UP COOKS

THE Lipton
SHORTCUT
COOKBOOK

OVER 300 NUTRITIOUS RECIPES FOR HURRY-UP COOKS

THE Lipton
SHORTCUT
COOKBOOK

MARGARET HOWARD

KEY PORTER·BOOKS

Canadian Cataloguing in Publication Data

Howard, Margaret
    The Lipton shortcut cookbook

Includes index.
ISBN 1-55013-012-9

1. Cookery. I. Thomas J. Lipton Inc. II. Title.

TX715.H69 1987   641.5'55   C87-093126-1

Key Porter Books Limited
70 The Esplanade
Toronto, Ontario
Canada M5E 1R2

Photography: Clive Webster
Food Stylist: Olga Truchan
Illustration: Nancy Kettles
Typesetting: Compeer Typographic Services Ltd.
Printing: Tri-Graphic Printing Ltd.
Printed and bound in Canada

91 92 93 94 95 8 7 6 5 4 3

CONTENTS

ACKNOWLEDGEMENTS

Writing this cookbook has given me a great deal of satisfaction and has allowed me to more fully express my personal recipe philosophy, which has now become the Lipton recipe philosophy—short recipes with few and readily available ingredients that are not too expensive. It has also given me an opportunity to provide today's busy consumer with many of the Lipton classic recipes plus many new and nutritious tested recipes for shortcut help in the kitchen.

To the home economists in the Lipton Consumer Test Kitchens, Pamela Hillman and Ryerson student, Elizabeth Linton, my thanks for their support in testing—and tasting—and testing again the recipes. And to Pam for the long hours she spent at the computer analyzing each recipe for its nutritional content. The CANDAT nutrition calculation system utilizing data from the Canadian Nutrient File from Health and Welfare Canada played a major role in this analysis. Thanks to freelance home economist Shirley Ann Holmes, who assisted with the microwave testing.

I am also grateful to food stylist Olga Truchan and photographer Clive Webster for their excellent photographs of many of the dishes. And to journalist friend Joyce Gillelan, who greatly helped me with introductory copy for the recipes.

My thanks to Laurie Coulter for carefully editing the manuscript and to Key Porter who proposed the idea and have encouraged and carefully guided me from start to finished manuscript.

And lastly to my company, Thomas J. Lipton, for providing me with the extra support and the extra time required to prepare a book of this size and scope.

INTRODUCTION

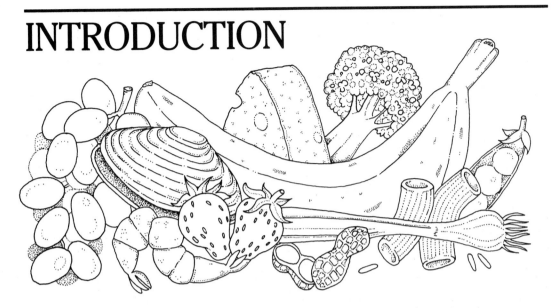

Since Sir Thomas Lipton first marketed the tea bag, the Lipton Company has been looking for ways to make every cook's life easier. This cookbook offers you the newest shortcuts and speediest recipes from the Lipton Consumer Test Kitchens. By using these recipes, you can prepare and cook delicious meals in minutes while giving the impression that you've been in the kitchen all day, or at least part of the day.

Cooking in minutes doesn't mean that you have to sacrifice quality and creativity in your cooking. However, it is necessary to have a collection of quick, nutritious recipes and to know every available shortcut. *The Lipton Shortcut Cookbook* provides you with both. So you can check your watch. Cook. Relax. And enjoy.

QUICK, HEALTHY RECIPES

I have chosen the recipes in this cookbook with the busy, active person in mind. Each recipe can be prepared in under thirty minutes, and many can be prepared in ten minutes or less. To help you plan your meals, estimated times for the preparation and final stages (cook, chill, marinate) have been given for each recipe.

Fast foods are frequently thought of as take-out foods. The foods I refer to as "fast foods" in this book are quick and easy to prepare but still very healthy and economical. Examples are fish, eggs and poultry, salads, cheese and pasta. Because today's consumer has a greater interest in nutrition, there is a particular emphasis on reducing cholesterol, saturated fats and sodium in many of the recipes. A nutritional analysis has been completed on each recipe on a per serving basis.

Part of the fun of working with food is the chance to be creative by developing new recipes and exploring new cuisines. Throughout the book there are new time-saver recipes for familiar comfort foods such as Cheesy Macaroni and Vegetables (page 48) along with easy exotic fare such as Oriental Marinated Pork (page 60) and Blueberry Velvet Cheesecake (page 133). As well, you'll find a few favorites of mine that I couldn't resist passing along as one cook to another.

Recipe Shortcuts
• Select recipes that best fit the available time.
• Before beginning a recipe, read it carefully and assemble ingredients and appliances.
• Start the longest preparation step first.

Preparation Shortcuts
• When you're grating cheese, grate more than you need and freeze it in labeled plastic bags in the quantities required for recipes. Do the same with chopped vegetables, bread crumbs and chopped nuts.
• Hard-cook eggs to keep in the refrigerator for sandwiches, salads or Spicy Deviled Egg Casserole (page 42). They'll keep up to one week.
• For your baking needs, toast nuts or coconut and keep a supply on your shortcut supply shelf.

SHORTCUT SUPPLY SHELF

In making the recipes in this book into meals, it is important to have a shortcut supply shelf. Supplies for your shelf have been selected to rescue you in all kinds of emergencies. Your long-lost relatives just dropped by — at supper time; your meeting with an out-of-town business client ran long—and you issued a spur-of-the-moment invitation for a home-cooked dinner; your best friend just landed in town — and you invited her for lunch. No matter what the emergency, no matter what you have in the refrigerator, a shortcut shelf will carry you through in style.

Shortcut Shelf Basics

Canned seafood (e.g. salmon, tuna, shrimp, crabmeat)
Puritan Flaked Chicken, Turkey and Ham
Fray Bentos Corned Beef
Frozen fish
Dried fruits (e.g. prunes, apples)
Dinner mixes (e.g. MexiCasa Enchilada Dinner, Taco Trio, Lipton Casserole bases)
Canned and frozen vegetables
Knox Unflavoured Gelatine
Herbal and Red Rose Tea bags
Lipton Noodles & Sauce, Pasta & Sauce and Rice & Sauce
Sour cream and/or plain yogurt
A modest spice and herb shelf

Bon Appétit Soup Mixes
Lipton Recipe and Soup Mixes
Lipton Cup.a.Soup Mixes
Jams and jellies (e.g. cranberry)
Canned and frozen fruit
Canned and frozen juices
Tomato sauce, paste and canned tomatoes
Graham, chocolate and vanilla wafers
Lucky Whip Dessert Topping Mix
Cocoa, semi- and unsweetened chocolate squares
Black Diamond Cheddar, Mozzarella, and Parmesan Cheeses
Assorted nuts (e.g. almonds, peanuts, walnuts)

STIR-FRY TO MICROWAVE

Although the conventional oven is ideal for cooking large quantities of food and complete meals, there are faster ways to get a meal on the table. Busy cooks can choose sautéing, frying or stir-frying. Or they can wrap food in foil, cook it at high oven temperatures and produce complete dishes in minutes with the added benefit of no clean-up.

The microwave is, of course, the newest, fastest and easiest method — for melting chocolate, softening cream cheese or margarine, thawing frozen food, preparing sauces and cooking complete meals in minutes. Preparation and dish washing are also easier because you can often cook and serve in the same dish. Microwave directions have been given for many recipes throughout the book; the recipes were tested in a 650 watt microwave oven.

Cooking Shortcuts

- When several people are expected for the same meal at different times, make up plates for each one and cover with plastic wrap. Simply pop the plate in the microwave for an instant meal.
- Microwave food on paper plates or paper toweling for easy clean-up.
- For a simple oven meal, put a roast in the oven along with a prepared-ahead vegetable and potato casserole, and a dessert.

ONE FOR THE MEAL, ONE FOR THE FREEZER

You can serve tasty nutritious meals quickly if you have prepared food, wrapped and labeled, in the freezer. While a frozen casserole is cooking, a salad can be completed, rolls warmed and a dessert unmolded. There are many recipes throughout the book for casseroles to freeze ahead. Desserts such as Raspberry Trifle (page 126) or Knox Ice Cream (page 138) can be made the night before as can Layered Garden Salad (page 30) or Cucumber Sour Cream Mousse (page 30).

What are the advantages of make-ahead cooking? Some dishes actually taste better when they're prepared the day before, so even if you don't have much freezer space, you can still use the make-ahead method. You can cook and bake when there are no time pressures. You can also save time and money by organizing your shopping into one weekly trip to take advantage of the specials. In addition, this method often means that you can use your modern equipment — the microwave, the food processor or blender, the freezer — to the best advantage so that they work together to ensure the best results in the least amount of time.

Make-ahead Shortcuts

- When you prepare casseroles, follow the old advice and make one for the meal and one for the freezer. Or make a triple batch of tomato-meat sauce at one time. Serve spaghetti one night; use it for chili with taco shells another night; and freeze one batch.
- Freeze leftovers in T.V. foil trays so individual meals are ready for those extra busy days.

TIME-SAVING MENU PLANNING

Many great meals are ruined because the recipes chosen were not compatible. There are five main areas in menu planning: color, texture, flavor, shape and temperature. A few guidelines follow and some of my favorite menus using recipes from this book.

It takes just as long to plan and cook a colorless meal as a colorful one. A classic example of dull meal planning is serving white fish with white boiled potatoes and creamed cauliflower. Zing up the plate and appetite by serving the same white fish with the vivid green of spinach and the bright red of tomatoes. Complement a soft food with a crisp food. Add a tossed salad, sprinkle toasted almonds on fish fillets and immediately the texture becomes more interesting.

Balance of flavors plays a major role in choosing foods to go together. Serve a tart food to accent bland flavors. Lemon meringue pie with fish is an example.

Beware of spicy ingredients. Serve one highly seasoned food at a meal—unless it's an ethnic meal. Make sure one flavor doesn't dominate a recipe. Some herbs and spices tend to overpower delicate meats (e.g. chicken and fish) masking their true flavor. Do not repeat flavors of foods from one course to another. If you use pork chops in a citrus sauce for the entrée, don't have an orange cake for dessert. Serve only one starchy food, other than bread, at each meal. Corn and potatoes, each starchy vegetables, are not complementary on the same plate. To end a meal, serve a heavy dessert with a light meal and a light dessert with a heavy meal.

Do not serve mixtures of foods, such as a casserole, with other mixtures of foods. A meat, pasta and vegetable casserole should be accompanied by a simple gelatine salad rather than a marinated vegetable salad. Serve cake or a melon wedge for dessert instead of a mixed fruit cup.

The contrast of hot and cold foods in the same menu provides greater interest—even in warm weather, a hot soup is a delicious introduction to a salad meal.

Garnishes are a quick addition to a meal that can lift it from ordinary to extraordinary. The secret is simplicity. Consider the plate the frame for the food and be sure the plate frames an attractive picture. In choosing garnishes, use many of the same considerations used in menu planning. Use garnishes that are complementary or contrasting in color, flavor or texture. One of the easiest ways to garnish is to arrange the foods themselves in a pleasing way. For an attractive lunch, line a plate with lettuce and heap shrimp around a tomato aspic mold.

Don't forget that a table setting can make your meal even more pleasant. Put the clutch of daisies your young daughter brings you in the middle of the table in a pretty vase. It can say more than the most elaborate centerpiece.

Above all, make food an adventure instead of a routine.

Menu Planning Shortcuts
- Consult shortcut menus (page 7).
- Choose recipes and plan meals for one week.
- Make a weekly shopping list for all your grocery needs.
- Reduce number of courses.
- Simplify preparation with cold meals.
- Use prepared foods, fast foods (fish, eggs and poultry, cheese and pasta) and leftovers.

NUTRIENT ANALYSIS OF RECIPES

To assess the nutrient rating of a single serving of food, we followed the guidelines of Canada's Food and Drug Regulations (D.01.005 and D.02.004). Each portion of food must provide the following amount of each nutrient to qualify as either a good or an excellent source.

Nutrient	Good Source	Excellent Source
Vitamin A (IU)	600	1200
Vitamin C (mg)	7.5	15.0
Thiamin (mg)	0.25	0.45
Riboflavin (mg)	0.40	0.75
Niacin (mg)	2.50	4.50
Calcium (mg)	150	300
Iron (mg)	2.0	4.0
Dietary fiber (g)	2.5–7.0	7.0+
Protein rating	20–39	40+

To qualify as having a low amount of fat, a single portion of food must have less than 2 g of fat.

Menus

MID-WEEK MENU FOR BUSY COOKS

Prepare ahead the night before.

Ten-Minute Tarragon Chicken / 67
Encore Potatoes / 93
Cucumber Sour Cream Mousse / 30
Orange Blossom Bundt Cake / 131

SHORTCUT FAMILY DINNER MENU

Cordon Bleu Economy Beef Rolls / 55
Broccoli Casserole / 98
Baked potatoes
Hot rolls
Green salad, with prepared salad / 36
dressing of your choice
Gingerbread Cake with
Fresh Fruit Sauce / 127

SHORTCUT BUT SPECIAL SUNDAY DINNER

Spicy Tomato Soup / 27
Rock Cornish hens *or* roasted poultry
Seasoned Vegetable Platter / 108
Festive Brandied Yams / 106
Shortcut Cheese Bread / 114
Asparagus-Tuna Crown / 32
Double Treat Chocolate Torte / 128

MEXICAN FIESTA MENU

Not-So-Sober Sangria / 148
Fiesta Nacho Appetizer / 11
Ensalada de Noche Buena / 32
Chicken or Turkey Mole / 73
Fiesta Rice / 92
Dessert Fruit Tacos / 130
Mexican Coffee / 148

FAMILY BIRTHDAY PARTY

Spicy Lemonade / 146
Lipton Onion Burgers / 54
Raw vegetable sticks
Birthday cake with
Celebration Frosting / 130

GALA OR SPECIAL OCCASION BUFFET

Glistening Champagne Punch / 147
Bloody Mary Dip / 15
Pacific Mousse / 76
Fillet of Beef with Parsley Stuffing / 58
Oriental Marinated Pork / 60
Apple Rice Pilaf / 90
Broccoli Casserole / 98
Layered Garden Salad / 30
Green salad with Vinaigrette Dressing / 39
Raspberry Trifle / 126
Chocolate Indulgence / 134

BRUNCH PARTY MENU

Sober Sangria / 148
or
Kiwifruit Daiquiris / 147
Classic Lipton Onion Dip *or* variations / 10
New Orleans Cajun-Style Eggs / 49
Meal-Time Scones / 116
or
Spiced Tea Bread / 114
Chocolate
or
Fresh Fruit Indulgence / 134

BACKYARD BARBECUE

Salmon in Seafood Marinade / 77
Primavera Pasta / 89
Green salad, with prepared salad / 36
dressing of your choice
Herbed Tomatoes / 105
Sherbet with Orange Liqueur Sauce / 132

EASY AND ELEGANT TEA PARTY MENU

Hot Pot Tea / 144
or
Tea Concentrate / 143
Perky Pinwheel Sandwiches — Wine, / 143
Cheese and Olive Filling
Tea-Time Sandwiches — Dilled Shrimp / 142
and Chicken Curry
Relish tray — celery, carrot, pickle slices,
pimiento-stuffed olives
Lemon Curd Tarts / 129
Coconut Shortbread / 119
Strawberries in Chocolate Cups / 129
Mints

DESSERT AND COFFEE PARTY

Unbaked Chocolate Marble / 132
Cheesecake
Blueberry Velvet Cheesecake / 133
Ecstasy / 137
Cheese and fruit tray
Dessert wines (port or sweet sherry)
Coffee garnished with cinnamon, orange
peel, lemon peel, whipped cream

HURRY-UP FAMILY OR COMPANY DINNER

One-Hour Beef Roast / 56
Caribbean Carrots / 101
Creamed Spinach / 104
Baked potatoes
Easy Elegant Bavarian Pie / 135

FRIDAY NIGHT MENU
(see cover)

Chicken Cacciatore / 67
Lipton Rice and Sauce — Polynesian
Snow peas
Glazed Fresh Fruit Tarts / 126

APPETIZERS

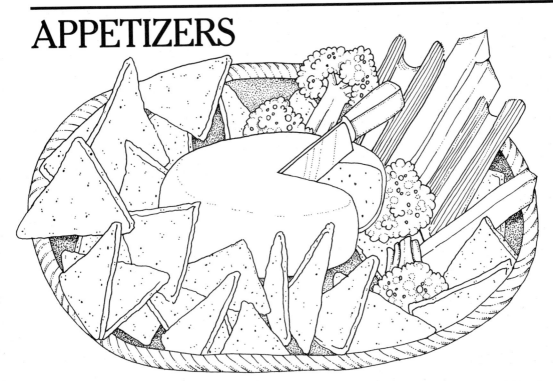

You can start a meal with a few appetizers or build a whole party around them. They're adaptable tidbits—freeze them and forget them until party time or make them at the last minute. If you are serving appetizers before a meal, keep them light and simple. Many a meal has been spoiled by too many appetizers. For a party you can indulge yourself with an array. In this section, you'll find hot and cold appetizers, and frozen and refrigerated appetizers to help you with year-round planning. Select them in different shapes, colors, textures and tastes, and arrange them attractively with creative garnishes. You'll have the best beginnings imaginable for your meals and parties.

QUICK SEASONING TIPS

Herbs and spices make a distinctive difference in your cooking. Experiment with them for new taste treats. However, use caution with strong spices such as cayenne pepper and curry; it's easier to add more spice than to try to correct an over-spiced dish. Cook with fresh herbs whenever you can. If you use dried herbs, adjust the quantities in a recipe as they are stronger than fresh herbs.

CREATIVE GARNISHING TIPS

Serve dippers and dips in an artistic way. Choose a handsome basket to hold a variety of colorful, attractive vegetables for dipping. Arrange radish roses on green onion stalks, supported with floral wire, mixed with long spiky carrot and zucchini fingers. Leafy celery stalks can be used for a contrast; fill in with cherry tomatoes, mushrooms and green pepper slices. For an edible vegetable centerpiece, serve dips in hollowed-out red or green pepper cups or a hollowed-out iceberg lettuce or red cabbage.

CLASSIC LIPTON ONION DIP

Preparation: about 5 minutes   Chill: about 30 minutes

The first dip many of us ever made or tasted is an all-time favorite — Lipton Onion Soup and sour cream. However, the Lipton Consumer Test Kitchens have developed some appealing new variations. Try them and see if your old favorite is still your favorite.

1	pouch Lipton Onion Soup	1	In a small bowl, combine soup and sour cream.
1	container (500 mL) dairy sour cream	1	Cover and chill until ready to serve.

Makes 2 cups (500 mL) dip.

Calories per 1 tbsp (15 mL): 27

VARIATIONS

To 1 cup (250 mL) dip add:

Cheesy Onion Dip: ½ cup (125 mL) grated Cheddar cheese.

Zesty Dip: 2 tbsp (25 mL) pickle relish and 1 tsp (5 mL) Worcestershire sauce.

Creamy Carrot–Onion Dip: ½ cup (125 mL) grated carrot, ½ cup (125 mL) chopped radishes and ¼ cup (50 mL) chopped fresh parsley.

Ginger Dip: 1 tsp (5 mL) ground ginger *or* 2 tsp (10 mL) finely chopped fresh ginger.

Blue Cheese Dip: ¼ lb (125 g) crumbled blue cheese and ¼ cup (50 mL) finely chopped walnuts.

Seafood Dip: ½ cup (125 mL) chopped cooked shrimp, clams *or* crabmeat, 2 tbsp (25 mL) chili sauce and 1–2 tsp (5–10 mL) horseradish.

Guacamole: 2 medium ripe avocados, mashed, 1 tbsp (15 mL) lemon juice and ¼ tsp (1 mL) hot pepper sauce.

Skinny Dip: In total recipe, replace part or all sour cream with plain yogurt.

ONION CHEESE BALL

Preparation: about 10 minutes   Chill: 1–2 hours

There's always another use for Classic Lipton Onion Dip. Here it lends its distinctive flavor to a cheese ball recipe. For a variation, a friend shapes it into a log and serves it on a black lacquer tray alongside a row of mildly flavored crackers. Or double all the ingredients (except the Lipton Onion Soup and sour cream) and make both a cheese ball and a cheese log; use one and freeze the other.

1	pouch Lipton Onion Soup	1	
1	container (500 mL) dairy sour cream *or* plain yogurt	1	
1	package (250 g) cream cheese, softened	1	
2 cups	grated Black Diamond Medium Cheddar Cheese	500 mL	
½ cup	finely crushed soda crackers	125 mL	
1 cup	chopped walnuts, divided Finely chopped fresh parsley	250 mL	

bowl, blend until smooth, 1 cup (250 mL) dip and the cheeses. Add crackers and half the nuts. Line a 4-cup (1 L) bowl with plastic wrap. Pack mixture into bowl; cover and chill. Unmold, cover with remaining nuts combined with parsley.

Makes 1 large or 2 small cheese balls.

TIPS: 1. Since the recipe calls for only half of the Classic Lipton Onion Dip, the remaining half can be served with chips or raw vegetables or as a topping for baked potatoes. 2. Cheese balls and spreads should stand at room temperature for at least ½ hour before serving.

Prepare Classic Lipton Onion Dip (see above) with soup mix and sour cream. In a medium

Calories per 1 tbsp (15 mL): 84

MEXICAN TURKEY PÂTÉ

Preparation: about 20 minutes   Chill: 1–2 hours

Leftover poultry can be turned into an easy, time-saving pâté. I frequently make several of these pâtés after Thanksgiving or Christmas and store them in the freezer. When I serve them months later, turkey has a fresh appeal.

2 cups	minced cooked turkey *or* chicken	500 mL
1	package MexiCasa Taco Seasoning Mix	1
¾ cup	water	175 mL
1	package (250 g) cream cheese, softened	1
	Chopped fresh parsley	
	Pimiento strips	

In a small saucepan, combine turkey, seasoning mix and water. Cook, uncovered, 10–12 minutes or until liquid is absorbed; cool thoroughly. Blend turkey mixture with cream cheese. Line a 2-cup (500 mL) mold or 2 smaller bowls with plastic wrap. Pack turkey-cheese mixture into mold; cover and chill 1–2 hours. Turn mold out onto a serving dish; garnish with parsley and pimiento strips

Makes 1 medium or 2 small pâtés.

TIP: When you line a bowl with plastic wrap, leave plenty of excess on the ends to cover the mixture once it is packed into the bowl. To remove, pull ends of wrap to loosen and it will slip away easily. Smooth creases on cheese with a spatula.

Calories per 1 tbsp (15 mL): 47

FIESTA NACHO APPETIZER

Preparation: about 10 minutes   Chill: 2–3 hours or overnight

Put a star beside this recipe — it's probably the best and easiest appetizer you'll ever prepare. Unmold it on a large serving platter and garnish with lettuce, cheese, tomato and green onions. Arrange nacho chips around the edge of the plate and "dip" in.

1	container (500 g) cottage cheese	1
2	packages (250 g) cream cheese, softened	2
1	package MexiCasa Taco Seasoning Mix	1
	Shredded lettuce, grated cheese, chopped tomato, chopped green onion	
	MexiCasa Nacho Chips	

In a blender or food processor, blend cottage cheese, cream cheese and seasoning mix until smooth. Line 2 small bowls with plastic wrap. Divide mixture evenly between bowls; cover and chill 2–3 hours or overnight, or freeze. Flavors improve with a few hours standing time. Garnish as desired at serving time.

Makes two 2-cup (500 mL) molds.

Calories per 1 tbsp (15 mL): 34

PESTO TORTA

Preparation: about 10 minutes   Chill: 1 hour

Once you try this spread, you'll want to serve it again and again. It can be molded in a bowl and later cut into wedges, or molded in small, individual loaf pans.

1	package (125 g) cream cheese, softened	1	Blend together cream cheese and margarine. Line a small mixing bowl with plastic wrap. Layer with one-third cheese mixture, half Pesto Sauce mixture. Repeat, ending with cheese; cover and chill until firm, about 1 hour, or freeze. Unmold and serve at room temperature with assorted crackers.
½ cup	margarine *or* butter	125 mL	
1 cup	Hurry-Up Pesto Sauce (recipe follows)	250 mL	

Makes one 2-cup (500 mL) mold.

Calories per 1 tbsp (15 mL): 57

PESTO SAUCES

Preparation: about 5 minutes

Basil is one of the herbs I grow in my garden, so I always have a fresh supply to make Pesto Sauces. Due to the amazing versatility of this sauce, I couldn't resist giving you recipes for two of my favorites: one using a hurry-up ingredient — onion soup mix — the other a new approach — lemons.

HURRY-UP PESTO SAUCE   Preparation: about 5 minutes

1	pouch Lipton Bon Appétit French Onion Soup	1	In a food processor or blender, blend soup mix, cheese, basil, nuts and oil until smooth. Store in refrigerator for up to 1 week.
¼ cup	Black Diamond Grated Parmesan Cheese	50 mL	
1 cup	packed fresh basil leaves, finely chopped	250 mL	**Makes 1 cup (250 mL) sauce.**
¼ cup	slivered almonds *or* pine nuts	50 mL	TIP: If you don't have fresh basil, you can substitute 2 tbsp (25 mL) dried basil and 1 cup (250 mL) fresh parsley.
2 tbsp	olive oil	25 mL	

Calories per 1 tbsp (15 mL): 37

LEMON PESTO SAUCE   Preparation: about 5 minutes

2 cups	packed fresh basil leaves	500 mL	**Makes ½ cup (125 mL) sauce.**
2	cloves garlic	2	
1 tbsp	EACH: olive oil, pine nuts *or* almonds	15 mL	
1 tsp	grated lemon rind	5 mL	TIPS: 1. Double these Pesto Sauces and freeze for later use. 2. They're fantastic spooned over hot cooked vegetables or hot pasta; blended with mayonnaise or in a salad dressing; spread on French bread; used as a zesty addition to soup; or served with poached or baked fish.
2 tbsp	fresh lemon juice	25 mL	

In a blender or food processor, combine all ingredients. Blend until smooth. Store in refrigerator for up to 1 week.

Calories per 1 tbsp (15 mL): 15   Vitamin C: Good   Low fat

GLAZED TERIYAKI CHICKEN WINGS

Preparation: about 10 minutes   Cook: about 35 minutes

Depending on the crowd you're expecting, you might want to halve this recipe; then again, if they're chicken-wing-lovers you might not. Either way, the wings will be glazed to a brown succulence. No one will guess they took only ten minutes to prepare.

2 lb	chicken wings, tips removed	1 kg
½ cup	brown sugar	125 mL
½ tsp	EACH: ginger, curry powder	2 mL
1–2	cloves garlic, minced	1–2
2 tbsp	all-purpose flour	25 mL
½ cup	soy sauce	125 mL
1 tbsp	vinegar	15 mL

Cut wings into 2 portions; place in a shallow baking pan. Mix brown sugar, seasonings, garlic and flour together; blend in soy sauce and vinegar and pour over wings. Bake at 400°F (200°C) 35–45 minutes. Stir occasionally. Remove from oven and serve hot in a chafing dish. May be frozen.

Microwave: Place prepared wings in an oblong baking dish. Pour sauce over wings. Cover with waxed paper and heat at HIGH (100%) 10–12 minutes or until fork tender; rearrange wings 2–3 times during cooking. Let stand 5–10 minutes.

Makes approximately 10 appetizer servings.

TIPS: 1. Because of the high sugar content, the chicken wings will burn easily. Check them frequently as they cook. 2. Same sauce may be used for spareribs, meatballs or ham cubes.

Calories per serving: 349

SEAFOOD-STUFFED MUSHROOMS

Preparation: about 10 minutes   Cook: 10 minutes

Mushroom lovers will follow this appetizer tray. Be sure there are enough to go around.

20–24	large mushrooms, cleaned	20–24
1	medium can crabmeat, shrimp, tuna or salmon	1
2 tbsp	mayonnaise	25 mL
⅛ tsp	EACH: Lawry's Seasoned Salt and Seasoned Pepper	0.5 mL
1 tbsp	lemon juice	15 mL
2 tbsp	minced chives or green pepper	25 mL

Remove stems from mushrooms. Combine remaining ingredients. Fill each mushroom with approximately 1 tsp (5 mL) mixture. Place on ungreased baking sheet. Bake at 400°F (200°C) 10 minutes.

Microwave: Prepare and fill mushrooms as directed above. Arrange 10–12 caps in a circle on paper towels on a round platter; cover with waxed paper. Heat at HIGH (100%) 4–5 minutes; rotate dish once or twice. Note: Smaller mushrooms can be placed in the center, since they cook faster than large ones.

Makes approximately 24 appetizers.

TIPS: 1. Don't fill mushrooms too full, or mixture will run out during baking. 2. Use chopped stems in casserole and other recipes.

Calories per mushroom: 20

MABEL'S CURRIED NUT NIBBLERS

Preparation: about 5 minutes   Cook: 25 minutes

Recently I attended a champagne brunch honoring Mabel Sherrill as The Home Economist of the Year. This recipe was developed by Mabel when she was a home economist with our company.

2 cups	walnut halves *or* whole blanched almonds	500 mL
1 tbsp	margarine *or* butter	15 mL
2 tsp	Lawry's Seasoned Salt	10 mL
¾ tsp	curry powder *or* chili powder	4 mL

Spread nuts in a shallow baking pan; dot with margarine. Bake at 350°F (180°C) 15–20 minutes or until golden; stir during baking to coat nuts; remove from oven. Blend seasonings together, sprinkle over nuts and stir. Return to oven and bake 5 minutes. Remove from oven; spread on paper towels to cool. Store in the refrigerator or freeze.

Microwave: In an oblong dish, melt margarine at HIGH (100%) 30–45 seconds. Thoroughly stir in seasonings and nuts. Heat, uncovered, at HIGH (100%) 4–5 minutes; stir twice. Spread on paper towels to cool.

Makes 2 cups (500 mL).

TIPS: 1. Make Nibblers in large quantities for hostess gifts. 2. Nuts sold in shops selling bulk food will often be less expensive and fresher.

Calories per ¼ cup (50 mL): 146

MAKE-AHEAD VEGETABLE DIP

Preparation: about 5 minutes   Chill: 2 hours

Combine Lipton 7 Vegetable Soup with sour cream for this instant vegetable dip. The Calico Seafood variation served in avocado halves makes an excellent appetizer or luncheon dish.

1	container (500 mL) dairy sour cream	1
1	pouch Lipton 7 Vegetable Soup	1

In a small bowl, combine soup and sour cream mix. Chill for at least 2 hours to allow flavors to blend.

Makes 2 cups (500 mL) dip.

Calories per 1 tbsp (15 mL): 26

VARIATIONS

Vegetable Yogurt Dip: Replace 1 cup (250 mL) sour cream with plain yogurt if you're a calorie-counting cook.
Vegetable Cheese Dip: Add ¼ cup (50 mL) grated Parmesan cheese *or* 1 cup (250 mL) grated Cheddar cheese.

Vegetable and Ginger Nut Dip: Add ⅓ cup (75 mL) chopped peanuts and ½ tsp (2 mL) ground ginger *or* 1 tsp (5 mL) finely chopped fresh ginger.
Calico Seafood Dip: Add 1 cup (250 mL) finely chopped cooked shrimp *or* crabmeat.

TIP: Leftovers may be used as tasty sandwich spreads.

BLOODY MARY DIP

Preparation: about 5 minutes   Chill: 1 hour

If a Bloody Mary is your favorite drink, chances are this will become your favorite dip. It was a success when it was developed in the Lipton Consumer Test Kitchens for a company reception and has been in demand ever since.

1	pouch Lipton Onion Soup	1
¼ cup	vodka *or* water	50 mL
½ cup	tomato sauce	125 mL
1	package (125 g) cream cheese, softened	1
1 cup	dairy sour cream	250 mL
¼ tsp	Tabasco sauce	1 mL
1 tsp	Worcestershire sauce	5 mL
1	head iceberg lettuce	1

In a small bowl, blend soup mix with vodka and tomato sauce. In a medium bowl, blend cream cheese with sour cream and sauces. Blend tomato mixture into creamed mixture and chill 1 hour. Serve in hollowed-out iceberg lettuce with assorted raw vegetable dippers (e.g. mushrooms, green or red pepper, carrots or celery sticks, snow peas, Belgian endive).

Makes approximately 2 cups (500 mL) dip.

TIP: Freeze leftover tomato sauce in ice cube trays. When frozen, place cubes in plastic bags for freezer storage.

Calories per 1 tbsp (15 mL): 35

CITRUS YOGURT DIP FOR FRUIT

Preparation: about 5 minutes   Chill: several hours

Sometimes I like to offer a variety of fresh fruits with dips. This refreshing pineapple and lemon dip, spiced with ginger, enhances the flavor of fresh fruit and treats your guests to a taste of summer anytime of the year.

¾ cup	plain yogurt	175 mL
¼ cup	pineapple *or* orange juice	50 mL
1 tsp	grated lemon peel	5 mL
¼–½ tsp	Lawry's Lemon Pepper	1–2 mL
¼ tsp	EACH: ground ginger, sugar	1 mL

In a small bowl, combine all ingredients until smooth. For best flavor, chill several hours or overnight before using. Serve with assorted fresh fruits (e.g. apple or pear wedges, strawberries, melon cubes, banana slices).

Makes approximately 1 cup (250 mL) dip.

Calories per 1 tbsp (15 mL): 9   Low fat

SQUARE MEATBALLS

Preparation: about 10 minutes   Cook: 15 minutes

This inspired time-saver recipe reduces preparation time by simply patting the meat into a pan and marking it into squares rather than rolling it into balls.

1 lb	lean ground beef	500 g
1	egg	1
¾ cup	fine soft bread crumbs	175 mL
¼ cup	finely minced onion	50 mL
2 tbsp	EACH: ketchup, water	25 mL
½ tsp	EACH: Lawry's Seasoned Salt and Seasoned Pepper Ripe olives, cocktail onions, cheese wedges, pickle slices	2 mL

In a medium bowl, combine all ingredients. On a jelly roll pan, shape into a rectangle 8 × 6 × ½ inch (20 × 15 × 1 cm); mark into squares.

Calories per meatball: 32, without garnish

Top each square with your favorite garnish. Bake at 400°F (200°C) 15 minutes. Cut into squares and serve with wooden toothpicks.

Microwave: Prepare meat, see above. Press into an 8-inch (2L) square baking pan. Top each square with your favorite garnish; cover, heat at HIGH (100%) 5–7 minutes. Turn dish after 4 minutes. Let stand, covered, 5 minutes before cutting into squares.

Makes 4 dozen.

TIP: Leftovers may be frozen for later use and then reheated.

HURRY-UP FONDUE

Preparation: about 10 minutes   Cook: 5 minutes

Soup mix hurries up this fondue preparation.

1	pouch Lipton Golden Onion Soup	1
1 cup	dry white wine	250 mL
½ cup	water	125 mL
2 cups	grated Swiss cheese French bread, cut into bite-size cubes	500 mL

In a medium saucepan, combine soup mix, wine and water. Bring to a boil, reduce heat and

Calories per ¼ cup (50 mL): 209

simmer, stirring constantly, until sauce is thickened, about 5 minutes. Gradually stir in cheese until melted. Pour into fondue pot or chafing dish. Serve hot with a basket of bread cubes to spear on fondue forks for dunking.

Microwave: In an 8-cup (2 L) covered casserole, combine soup mix, wine and water. Heat at HIGH (100%) 3–4 minutes or until bubbles form; stir once. Add cheese and heat at MEDIUM (50%) 2–3 minutes stirring every minute until cheese is melted.

Makes approximately 2 cups (500 mL).

VARIATION

Pesto Fondue: Just before serving, swirl one of the Pesto Sauces (page 12) over surface in a figure eight pattern.

JALAPEÑO PEPPER JELLY

Preparation: about 10 minutes   Cook: about 5 minutes

This medium-hot pepper jelly can be made any time of the year. Use it as an appetizer by spreading crackers with cooling cream cheese and a dab of jelly or serve it as an accompaniment to pork, ham or chicken.

¾ cup	chopped MexiCasa Jalapeño Peppers	175 mL
¾ cup	chopped sweet green *or* red pepper	175 mL
1¼ cups	cider vinegar, divided	300 mL
6 cups	sugar	1.5 L
1	bottle (170 mL) liquid pectin	1
	Red or green food coloring	

In a blender or food processor, combine peppers and ¼ cup (50 mL) vinegar; blend until liquid consistency. In a medium saucepan, combine pepper mixture, sugar and remaining vinegar. Bring to a boil, remove from heat and skim surface. Stir in pectin and food coloring; return to a boil for 1 minute. Remove from heat, fill sterilized jars and seal with paraffin.

Makes 4 cups (1 L).

Calories per 1 tbsp (15 mL): 9

EASY CAJUN SHRIMP

Preparation: about 5 minutes   Cook: 10 minutes

One of the newest trends in cooking is colorful, spicy Cajun food. This recipe can be served on noodles or rice as an entrée. It's also a winner as an appetizer or "little meal," especially when served on large scallop shells garnished with lemon and fresh basil.

1½ cups	shelled, deveined shrimp	375 mL
1	pouch Lipton Bon Appétit Minestrone Soup	1
1	can (19 oz/540 mL) tomatoes, undrained	1
½ cup	water	125 mL
¼ tsp	EACH: chili powder, basil	1 mL
1 tbsp	Lemon juice	15 mL
	Lemon wedges	
	Fresh basil *or* parsley	

Rinse shrimp in cold water; drain thoroughly. In a medium saucepan, combine soup mix, tomatoes, water, chili powder, basil and lemon juice.

Bring to a boil, reduce heat, cover and simmer 5 minutes. Add shrimp, continue simmering 5 minutes or until shrimp are tender. Serve shrimp and sauce garnished with lemon wedges and sprigs of fresh basil or parsley.

Microwave: In a 4-cup (1 L) covered casserole, combine soup mix, tomatoes, seasonings and lemon juice (omit water). Heat at HIGH (100%) 6–7 minutes. Add shrimp; heat at HIGH 2–3 minutes. Stir once. Let stand 5 minutes.

Makes 3–4 appetizer or 2 main course servings.

Calories per serving: 135   Vitamin C: Excellent   Vitamin A and iron: Good   Low fat

SOUPS

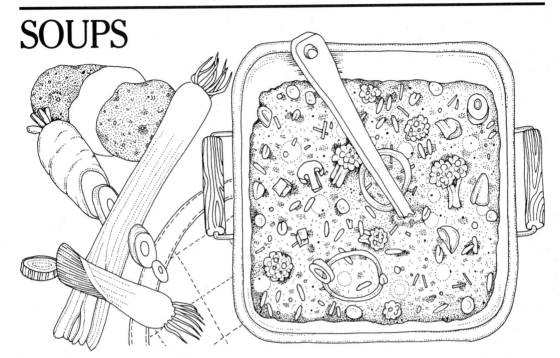

These are lunch and supper favorites— some with an international flair. All are prepared quickly with step-saving ingredients. You can make up a soup mix in minutes or simmer a soup kettle on the back of the stove. A quick convenient bouillon base for soup can be made with OXO Beef, Chicken or Onion Cubes. A meat extract, now known as OXO, was introduced in 1861 and is still popular as a regular item on shopping lists around the world. It was one of the first convenience foods. Its virtues as an aid to health and strength were extolled by such diverse people as Florence Nightingale, the Second Duke of Wellington, and Sir Henry Stanley, the explorer.

QUICK SEASONING TIPS

The distinctive tastes and smells of herbs add to our enjoyment of homemade soup. Next time you're making soup, use a French method of cooking by adding a bouquet garni made with fresh or dried herbs. For a fresh bouquet garni, fill a stalk of celery with sprigs of chervil, parsley, thyme and a bay leaf. Cover with a second stalk of celery, tie them together with white string and add them to the soup. For a dried herb bouquet garni, tie a selection of herbs into a cheesecloth bag or place in a stainless steel tea ball. An excellent combination is chives, tarragon, parsley and basil.

CREATIVE GARNISHING TIPS

Float thin lemon or cucumber slices on clear soups. Snipped parsley or chives, and chopped green peppers are also attractive. For cream soups, try croutons, crumbled bacon, sprigs of parsley, toasted almonds, shredded cheese or crushed corn chips. Hot soups usually have heartier garnishes than cold soups. Choose a garnish that complements the soup in taste, texture and color.

CUCUMBER VICHYSSOISE

Preparation: about 10 minutes   Cook: 5 minutes   Chill: about 1 hour

The use of Lipton Cream of Leek Soup makes the preparation of this vichyssoise fast and simple. It's even more refreshing served in hollowed-out cucumbers.

1	package Lipton Bon Appétit Cream of Leek Soup	1
1½ cups	cold water	375 mL
1 cup	peeled, seeded and cubed cucumber	250 mL
1 cup	light cream Chopped chives	250 mL

In a medium saucepan, stir soup mix into water. Bring to a boil, stirring constantly. Immediately reduce heat to simmer. Stir frequently for 5 minutes, uncovered. Remove from heat, cool slightly. Place in a blender, add cucumber and purée until smooth. Stir in cream and chill. Garnish with chopped chives.

Makes approximately 3 cups (750 mL).

Calories per serving: 200

VARIATION

Chilled Vichyssoise: As above but omit cucumber.

Makes 2 cups (500 mL).

CHILLED WHITE GAZPACHO

Preparation: about 10 minutes   Chill: about 1 hour

Gazpacho is a cold vegetable soup-salad of Spanish origin. The "salad" tops the soup rather than being combined with it. Diced red tomatoes, chopped green onions and slivered golden almonds are dramatic sprinkled on the surface of the white soup.

2	English cucumbers, peeled and diced	2
1 cup	chicken broth	250 mL
2 tbsp	white wine vinegar	25 mL
¼ tsp	Lawry's Garlic Powder	1 mL
1 tsp	Lawry's Seasoned Salt	5 mL
2 cups	dairy sour cream *or* yogurt	500 mL
	Diced tomatoes, chopped green onions, slivered almonds	

In a food processor or blender, purée cucumber and chicken broth until smooth. Add remaining ingredients and blend well. Chill before serving. Garnish with tomatoes, green onions and slivered almonds.

Makes 4 servings.

TIPS: 1. Chicken broth can be made instantly from 1 OXO Chicken Bouillon Cube and 1 cup (250 mL) boiling water. 2. For an exciting addition, stir in a spoonful of Lemon Pesto Sauce (page 12)

Calories per serving: 219, without garnish   Vitamins A and C; calcium: Good

CHUNKY GAZPACHO

Preparation: about 15 minutes   Chill: about 1 hour

Were the Spanish thinking of Chunky Gazpacho soup when they conceived the proverb: "Of soup and love, the first is best"?

¼ tsp	EACH: garlic powder, oregano	1 mL
1	package MexiCasa Taco Seasoning Mix	1
1½ cups	tomato juice	375 mL
4–6	fresh tomatoes, peeled and chopped	4–6
1	medium cucumber, peeled and chopped	1
¼ cup	EACH: minced green pepper, minced green onion	50 mL
2 tbsp	olive oil	25 mL
1 tbsp	vinegar *or* white wine vinegar	15 mL
	Lawry's Seasoned Pepper, to taste	

In a large bowl, blend garlic powder, oregano and seasoning mix with tomato juice. Add tomatoes, cucumber, green pepper, green onion, olive oil, vinegar and pepper; mix thoroughly. Chill before serving.

Makes 5-6 servings.

TIP: For a smoother version, this soup may be puréed.

Calories per serving: 114   Vitamins A and C: Excellent   Iron and fiber: Good

CURRIED CARROT SOUP

Preparation: 20 minutes   Cook: 20 minutes

A soup that can be served either hot or cold, is a useful year-round addition to your recipes. When serving, swirl sour cream into the soup and top with chopped chives or finely grated carrots.

4	OXO Chicken Bouillon Cubes	4
2	OXO Onion Bouillon Cubes	2
4 cups	boiling water	1 L
4 cups	thinly sliced carrots	1 L
1	strip of lemon peel	1
2 tsp	sugar	10 mL
½ tsp	curry powder	2 mL
¼ cup	light cream	50 mL
½ cup	dairy sour cream	125 mL
	Chopped chives *or* grated carrots	

In a large saucepan, dissolve bouillon cubes in boiling water. Add carrots, lemon peel, sugar and curry powder. Bring to a boil, then reduce heat, cover and simmer about 20 minutes until carrots are tender. In partially covered blender or food processor, purée until smooth. Return to saucepan and heat through. Stir in cream and season to taste. May be frozen. Garnish with sour cream, chives or carrots.

Microwave: In an 8-cup (2 L) covered casserole, heat water at HIGH (100%) until boiling. Add bouillon cubes; stir to dissolve. Add carrots, lemon peel, sugar and curry powder. Heat, covered, at HIGH 4–5 minutes or until boiling. Heat at MEDIUM (50%) 10–13 minutes until carrots are tender. Purée as above. Return to casserole, heat at HIGH 1–2 minutes; stir in cream and season. Serve as above.

Makes approximately 6 servings.

Calories per serving: 120, without garnish   Vitamin A: Excellent   Fiber: Good

BORSCHT

Preparation: about 10 minutes   Cook: 20 minutes

Borscht is the most famous of the Slav soups. There are as many recipes as cooks, but the soup is always served with a sour cream garnish.

5	OXO Beef Bouillon Cubes	5
4 cups	boiling water	1 L
3	large beets, peeled and coarsely grated	3
½ cup	finely chopped onions	125 mL
1 tbsp	lemon juice	15 mL
	Dairy sour cream	

In a large saucepan, dissolve bouillon cubes in boiling water. Add remaining ingredients, except sour cream. Reduce heat, cover and simmer 20 minutes or until raw vegetables are tender. May be frozen. Garnish with a large dollop of sour cream.

Calories per serving: 32, without sour cream

Microwave: In an 8-cup (2 L) covered casserole, heat water at HIGH (100%) until boiling. Add bouillon cubes; stir to dissolve. Add remaining ingredients except sour cream. Heat, covered, at MEDIUM (50%) 15–20 minutes or until raw vegetables are tender. Let stand, covered, 5 minutes. Garnish with sour cream.

Makes approximately 4–5 servings.

TIP: Although borscht is usually served as a hot soup, it is equally good when it is served cold.

MEXICAN VEGETABLE SOUP

Preparation: about 10 minutes   Cook: 15 minutes

Pass small bowls of garnishes with the soup and let your guests serve themselves.

½ lb	ground beef	250 g
1	pouch Lipton Tomato Vegetable Soup	1
1	can (7½ oz/213 mL) tomato sauce	1
2 cups	water	500 mL
1	can (14 oz/398 mL) red kidney beans	1
1 cup	frozen corn kernels	250 mL
1 cup	diced zucchini (optional)	250 mL
1½–2 tsp	chili powder	7–10 mL
1 tsp	oregano	5 mL
½ tsp	garlic powder	2 mL
	Grated Black Diamond Cheddar Cheese, chopped tomatoes, sliced green onions, ripe olives, sour cream, and MexiCasa Nacho Chips	

In a Dutch oven or large heavy saucepan, brown ground beef; drain fat. Add soup mix, tomato sauce, water, kidney beans, corn, zucchini and seasonings; mix well. Bring to a boil, then reduce heat, cover and simmer 15 minutes. Garnish as desired. May be frozen.

Microwave: In an 8-cup (2 L) covered casserole, crumble ground beef. Heat at HIGH (100%) 3–4 minutes; break up and drain. Add remaining ingredients; mix well. Heat, covered, at HIGH 3–5 minutes or until boiling. Heat at MEDIUM (50%) 5–8 minutes. Let stand, covered, 5 minutes.

Makes 4–5 servings.

Calories per serving: 319, without garnish   Fiber and iron: Excellent   Vitamins A and C: Good

CHEDDAR CHEESE 'N ONION SOUP

Preparation: about 10 minutes   Cook: about 10 minutes

If you have any assorted leftover cheese in your refrigerator, you can use it to supplement the Cheddar cheese called for in this recipe.

1 tbsp	margarine *or* butter	15 mL
¼ cup	minced onion	50 mL
2–3 tbsp	all-purpose flour	25–45 mL
2 cups	scalded milk	500 mL
2 cups	EACH: half and half cream, chicken broth	500 mL
2 cups	grated Black Diamond Extra Old Cheddar Cheese	500 mL
1 tsp	Lawry's Seasoned Salt	5 mL
1	medium zucchini, grated (optional)	1

In a medium saucepan, melt margarine and sauté onion. Add flour and stir to make a roux. Gradually add scalded milk, cream and broth; stir until smooth and thickened. Heat to just below boiling. Stir in cheese and seasoned salt; cook over very low heat until cheese melts. Soup may be frozen at this stage. Sprinkle zucchini over top of soup before serving.

Makes 4–6 servings.

Calories per serving: 343   Calcium: Excellent   Vitamin A and riboflavin: Good

HEARTY ITALIAN SOUP

Preparation: about 10 minutes   Cook: 25 minutes

This soup is given added zest with the addition of hot Italian sausage. A lover of Italian food I know says this spicy soup is addictive.

¾ lb	hot Italian sausage, sliced	375 g
½	medium green pepper, chopped	½
1	medium onion, chopped	1
1	can (19 oz/540 mL) tomatoes, broken up	1
1	can (7½ oz/213 mL) tomato sauce	1
2 cups	water	500 mL
½ tsp	garlic powder	2 mL
1	pouch Lipton Chicken Noodle Soup	1
½ cup	grated Black Diamond Mozzarella Cheese	125 mL

In a Dutch oven or large heavy saucepan, brown sausage, green pepper and onion; drain. Add tomatoes, tomato sauce, water and garlic powder. Bring to a boil, then reduce heat, cover and simmer 15 minutes. Add soup mix; simmer, covered, 5–7 minutes longer. May be frozen at this stage. Sprinkle each serving with grated Mozzarella cheese.

Microwave: In an 8-cup (2 L) covered casserole, combine sausage, green pepper and onion. Heat at HIGH (100%) 5–6 minutes; drain. Add tomatoes, tomato sauce, water and garlic powder. Heat at HIGH 5–7 minutes; stir once. Add soup mix; cover; heat at HIGH 4–5 minutes. Let stand, covered, 5 minutes. Garnish with Mozzarella cheese.

Makes 4–5 servings.

Calories per serving: 430   Vitamins A and C; thiamin: Excellent   Calcium and iron: Good

CHICKEN NOODLE LENTIL SOUP

Preparation: about 10 minutes   Cook: 30 minutes

The fact that lentils are a good source of protein and fiber is suggested in this Hindu proverb: "Rice is good, but lentils are my life."

1 cup	lentils	250 mL
5 cups	water	1.25 L
1	can (7½ oz/213 mL) tomato sauce	1
1	bay leaf	1
1 tsp	Lawry's Seasoned Pepper	5 mL
½ tsp	salt	2 mL
1	potato, peeled and chopped	1
2	celery stalks, chopped	2
2 tsp	oregano	10 mL
1	pouch Lipton Chicken Noodle Soup	1

In a large saucepan, combine all ingredients except soup mix. Bring to a boil, then reduce heat, cover and simmer 25 minutes. Add soup mix, cook 5 minutes longer.

Microwave: In an 8-cup (2 L) covered casserole, combine all ingredients except soup mix. Heat at HIGH (100%) 6–8 minutes or until boiling. Heat at MEDIUM (50%) 12–15 minutes; stir frequently. Add soup mix; heat at MEDIUM 5 minutes or until vegetables are tender. Let stand, covered, 5 minutes.

Makes 6–7 servings.

Calories per serving: 124   Vitamin C: Good

FRENCH ONION SOUP

Preparation: about 5 minutes   Cook: about 10 minutes

When you use Lipton Onion Soup, this specialty of Paris can be prepared in minutes—without tears.

1	pouch Lipton Onion Soup	1
4 cups	water	1 L
⅓ cup	white wine (optional)	75 mL
4	slices French bread, toasted	4
4	Swiss cheese slices	4
¼ cup	Black Diamond Grated Parmesan Cheese	50 mL

Prepare soup mix according to package directions. If desired, add wine after simmering time. Ladle soup into 4 ovenproof bowls; top with toasted bread and Swiss cheese. Sprinkle with Parmesan cheese. Broil until cheese is golden brown.

Makes 4 servings.

TIPS: 1. When choosing a soup, harmonize it with the rest of the menu. For example, serve French Onion Soup with crusty bread, a green salad and Orange Blossom Bundt Cake (page 131). 2. Warm your knife in hot water before slicing cheese and it will slice easily.

Calories per serving: 201   Calcium: Excellent

HOT DIGGITY DOG TOMATO SOUP

Preparation: about 5 minutes   Cook: 10 minutes

By using wieners and macaroni in this soup, you're assured of a winning combination for children's lunches.

1	pouch Lipton Tomato Vegetable Soup	1
4 cups	water	1 L
1/3 cup	macaroni	75 mL
4	wieners, sliced diagonally Grated Black Diamond Cheddar Cheese (optional)	4

In a medium saucepan, combine soup mix and water. Bring to a boil, add macaroni and cook, covered, 5 minutes. Add wieners, cook another 5 minutes. Sprinkle with grated Cheddar cheese if desired.

Microwave: In an 8-cup (2 L) covered casserole, combine soup mix and water. Heat at HIGH (100%) 3–4 minutes or until boiling. Add macaroni, heat at HIGH 3–4 minutes. Add wieners and heat at HIGH another 2–3 minutes. Let stand, covered, 5 minutes.

Makes 4–5 servings.

TIP: Any leftover soup? Add leftover dinner vegetables and serve tomorrow for another variation.

Calories per serving: 247, without grated cheese   Vitamin C: Good

TUNA CHOWDER

Preparation: about 10 minutes   Cook: 20 minutes

A steaming bowl of chowder on a cold winter's night is a soothing start to a meal.

2	medium carrots, thinly sliced	2
1/2 cup	chopped celery	125 mL
2	medium potatoes, peeled and cubed	2
1	can (14 oz/398 mL) tomatoes, undrained	1
1	pouch Lipton Onion Soup	1
1/8 tsp	pepper	0.5 mL
1 1/2 cups	water	375 mL
1	can (7 oz/198 g) tuna, drained and flaked	1
1/2 cup	frozen peas	125 mL
1 cup	milk	250 mL

In a medium saucepan, combine all ingredients except frozen peas and milk. Bring to a boil, then reduce heat, cover and simmer 10–15 minutes or until vegetables are just tender. Add frozen peas and milk; simmer 5 minutes longer. May be frozen.

Microwave: In an 8-cup (2 L) covered casserole, combine all ingredients except frozen peas and milk. Heat at HIGH (100%) 8–10 minutes or until boiling. Heat at MEDIUM (50%) 10–12 minutes or until vegetables are just tender. Add frozen peas and milk. Let stand, covered, 5 minutes.

Makes 4–5 servings.

Calories per serving: 243   Fiber, vitamins A and C: Excellent   Iron: Good

MANHATTAN CLAM CHOWDER

Preparation: about 5 minutes   Cook: 5 minutes

Clam chowder lovers forever argue the merits of adding or not adding tomatoes. Try this quick, easy chowder recipe and you'll agree that tomatoes add a great taste.

1	pouch Lipton Bon Appétit Cream of Leek Soup	1
1	can (14 oz/398 mL) tomatoes, undrained	1
1	can (5 oz/142 g) clams, undrained	1
1 cup	water	250 mL

In a medium saucepan, combine all ingredients. Bring to a boil, stirring constantly. Imme-diately reduce heat, simmer uncovered for 5 minutes, stirring frequently.

Microwave: In a 6-cup (1.5 L) covered casserole, combine all ingredients. Heat at HIGH (100%) 4–5 minutes or until boiling; stir twice. Heat at MEDIUM (50%) 2–3 minutes. Let stand, covered, 5 minutes.

Makes 4 servings.

Calories per serving: 84   Vitamin C: Excellent   Vitamin A and iron: Good

CHILI ALBÓNDIGAS

Preparation: about 15 minutes   Cook: 20 minutes

This Mexican meatball soup, served with crusty bread, can be a meal in itself. Or served in small cups it's a nice beginning for a meal to accompany tacos.

1 lb	ground beef	500 g
¼ cup	rice	50 mL
¼ cup	ice water	50 mL
1½ tsp	Lawry's Seasoned Salt, divided	7 mL
1	package MexiCasa Taco Seasoning Mix	1
1½ cups	water	375 mL
1	can (14 oz/398 mL) tomatoes, undrained	1
1	can (14 oz/398 mL) red kidney beans, undrained	1
½ cup	slivered onion	125 mL
1	bay leaf	1

Combine ground beef, rice, water and 1 tsp (5 mL) seasoned salt; mix lightly. Form into 20 meatballs. In a large saucepan, mix together seasoning mix, water and tomatoes. Add beans, onion, bay leaf and remaining ½ tsp (2 mL) seasoned salt. Bring to a boil; add meatballs. Reduce heat, cover and simmer 20 minutes, stirring occasionally. May be frozen.

Makes 5 servings of 4 meatballs each.

Calories per serving: 418   Fiber and iron: Excellent   Vitamin C and protein: Good

Clockwise: Glistening Champagne Punch (page 147); Glazed Teriyaki Chicken Wings (page 13); Pesto Torta (page 12); Seafood-Stuffed Mushrooms (page 13); Vegetable and Ginger Nut Dip (page 14)

SPICY TOMATO SOUP

Preparation: about 5 minutes   Cook: 5 minutes

A surprise ingredient in this soup is Italian salad dressing combined with tomato juice. Garnish with thin lemon slices for an easy, elegant start to your meal.

1	package WishBone Zesty Italian Dressing	1
1	can (48 oz/1.36 L) tomato juice	1
2 tsp	parsley flakes	10 mL
Dash	EACH: Worcestershire and Tabasco sauce	Dash
	Lemon slices	

Prepare dressing according to package directions. In a medium saucepan, combine all ingredients, using ¾ cup (175 mL) prepared dressing. Bring to a boil, then reduce heat and simmer 5 minutes. Serve warm as a soup or beverage. Garnish with lemon slices.

Microwave: Prepare salad dressing. In a 6-cup (1.5 L) casserole, combine all ingredients, using ¾ cup (175 mL) prepared dressing. Heat at HIGH (100%) 5–7 minutes or until boiling. Heat at MEDIUM (50%) 2–3 minutes.

Makes 6 servings.

Calories per serving: 53   Vitamins A and C: Excellent

VARIATION

Spiked Spicy Tomato Soup: Add ¼ cup (50 mL) dry sherry.

EGG DROP SOUP

Preparation: about 5 minutes   Cook: about 5 minutes

Also known as Soup of the Gods, Egg Drop Soup is one of the most popular soups in China. Most of their soups use clear broth as a base. Take a shortcut by using bouillon cubes.

4	OXO Beef *or* Chicken Bouillon Cubes	4
4 cups	boiling water	1 L
¼ tsp	ginger	1 mL
2	eggs, beaten	2
¼ cup	chopped fresh parsley	50 mL

In a medium saucepan, dissolve bouillon cubes in boiling water. (If using OXO Chicken Bouillon Cubes, omit ginger.) Add ginger and beaten eggs; stir constantly, over low heat, until eggs separate into shreds. Ladle into soup cups. Sprinkle with parsley.

Makes 6 servings.

Calories per serving: 34

Clockwise: Chilled White Gazpacho (page 20); Cheddar Cheese 'n Onion Soup (page 23); Mexican Vegetable Soup (page 22)

SALADS

Usually salads are thought of as a last-minute food. In fact, molded, layered and marinated salads should be made the night before. A tossed salad can be made into a make-ahead one by putting dressing into a salad bowl and marinating chunky vegetables like tomatoes, cucumbers and carrots. Place the greens on top and the vegetables will lift them above the dressing. If you prefer to make a tossed salad just before serving, you can make the preparation easier by washing and drying greens in the morning, chopping the required amounts of vegetables and storing them in plastic bags. Simplify salad dressing preparations by preparing a variety and storing them in the refrigerator. Then select one to complement the salad and your meal.

QUICK SEASONING TIPS

Herbs and salads were made for each other and that's even more true for salad dressings. To add an interesting variety, make your own herb vinegars. The most common ones are: tarragon, mint, basil, marjoram, dill and caraway. They are easily made by bringing vinegar to a boil and pouring it over fresh herbs. You can use one variety of herb or a combination. Cover tightly and infuse for ten days or longer if you want a stronger flavor.

CREATIVE GARNISHING TIPS

One of the easiest ways to achieve spectacular cooking results is to serve a molded salad that is attractively garnished. Repeat some of the salad ingredients for garnishes. For instance, for Cucumber Sour Cream Mousse (page 30), use cucumber twists (made like lemon twists) with cherry tomatoes or ripe olives and Italian broadleaf parsley. Layered and marinated salads need no garnish because they are spectacular as is. Remember to use vegetable garnishes with vegetable salads. They can be as complicated as a tomato rose or as simple as tomato wedges around the edge of the salad.

LAYERED GARDEN SALAD

Preparation: 20 minutes   Chill: 3–4 hours

This prepared-ahead salad is a dieter's dream because it is so low in calories.

1	medium onion, chopped	1
½ cup	chopped cucumber	125 mL
1	container (500 g) low-fat cottage cheese	1
¼ cup	Black Diamond Grated Parmesan Cheese	50 mL
1 tbsp	Becel Margarine	15 mL
1	large green pepper, finely chopped	1
2 tsp	lemon juice	10 mL
¼ tsp	Tabasco sauce	1 mL
2	tomatoes, chopped Lettuce	2

In a small bowl, combine onion and cucumber. In a food processor or blender, cream cottage cheese, Parmesan cheese and margarine until smooth. Add to onion and cucumber. In a second bowl, combine green pepper, lemon juice and Tabasco. In a 6-cup (1.5 L) clear glass bowl, layer half the chopped tomatoes, half the cottage cheese mixture, and half the green pepper mixture; repeat layers. Cover and chill 3–4 hours. Serve on a bed of lettuce.

Makes 4 servings.

Calories per serving: 163   Vitamin C: Excellent   Vitamin A: Good

CUCUMBER SOUR CREAM MOUSSE

Preparation: about 10 minutes   Chill: 2 hours

Capture the cool freshness of summer in this spectacular and elegant showpiece. Of course, it can be prepared ahead of time.

1	pouch Knox Unflavoured Gelatine	1
1 tbsp	sugar	15 mL
¼ cup	cold water	50 mL
1 cup	boiling water	250 mL
½ tsp	EACH: salt, dry mustard, Worcestershire sauce	2 mL
Dash	pepper	Dash
1 tbsp	EACH: minced fresh parsley, chopped fresh dill	15 mL
1 tbsp	vinegar	15 mL
¼ cup	lemon juice	50 mL
1	large English cucumber, unpeeled, shredded	1
1	green onion, minced	1
1 cup	dairy sour cream *or* low-fat yogurt	250 mL

In a small bowl, combine gelatine and sugar. Add cold water, allow to soften 2–3 minutes; add boiling water, stir constantly until gelatine is completely dissolved. Stir in seasonings, parsley, dill, vinegar and lemon juice. Chill until consistency of unbeaten egg white. Add cucumber, green onion and sour cream. Pour into a lightly oiled 4-cup (1 L) mold. Chill 2 hours until set.

Makes 6 servings.

TIP: If gel mixture becomes too firm at the point of adding other ingredients, place mixture in a saucepan over low heat and stir just until the mixture returns to a smooth-textured liquid state. Repeat the chilling process to the desired stage and the mixture will re-set.

Calories per serving: 125   Fiber; vitamins A and C; iron: Excellent

PESTO PICNIC SALAD

Preparation: about 20 minutes   Chill: 1–2 hours

A supply of pesto sauce in your freezer makes quick work of many recipes from appetizers to entrées to salads.

4 cups	cooked fusilli *or* rigatoni pasta	1 L
1	tomato, coarsely chopped	1
½ cup	EACH: diced cooked carrots, cooked peas	125 mL
½ cup	EACH: sliced black olives, Black Diamond Grated Parmesan Cheese	125 mL
¾ cup	Pesto Salad Dressing (recipe follows)	175 mL

In a large salad bowl, combine all ingredients. Chill 1–2 hours.

Makes 6 servings.

Calories per serving: 417   Fiber: Good   Vitamin A: Excellent

PESTO SALAD DRESSING   Preparation Time: under 5 minutes

For a simple salad, drizzle this basil dressing over tomato slices. It also adds zest to Pesto Picnic Salad.

2–3 tbsp	Hurry-Up Pesto Sauce (page 12)	10–15 mL
⅔ cup	vegetable *or* olive oil	150 mL
¼ cup	vinegar	50 mL
1 tbsp	sugar	15 mL

Add Pesto Sauce to vegetable oil, vinegar and sugar. Refrigerate until ready to use.

Makes ¾ cup (175 mL).

Calories per 1 tbsp (15 mL): 126

FRESH CITRUS PASTA SALAD

Preparation: 20 minutes   Chill: about 2 hours

The color and piquancy of citrus fruit is a pleasing contrast to pasta. Serve this unusual salad all year long.

2 cups	water	450 mL
1	package Lipton Pasta & Sauce – Creamy Bacon Carbonara	1
¼ cup	vegetable oil	50 mL
2 tbsp	fresh lemon juice	25 mL
½ tsp	grated lemon rind	2 mL
1 tsp	Dijon mustard	5 mL
1	small clove garlic, minced	1
2	oranges, peeled, cut in slices and quartered	2
½ cup	sliced celery	125 mL
1	green onion, thinly sliced	1

In a medium saucepan, bring water to a boil. Stir in pasta and sauce mix. Simmer, uncovered, over medium heat, 10 minutes; stir occasionally. Remove from heat. Let stand, covered, 3–5 minutes to allow sauce to thicken. In a small bowl, combine oil, lemon juice and rind, mustard and garlic. Pour over cooked pasta; allow to cool. Add remaining ingredients. Chill about 2 hours.

Makes 5–6 servings.

Calories per serving: 220   Vitamin C: Excellent   Vitamin A: Good

ASPARAGUS–TUNA CROWN

Preparation: about 15 minutes   Chill: 2 hours

When asparagus comes into season, it deserves this royal treatment.

2	pouches Knox Unflavoured Gelatine	2
½ cup	cold water	125 mL
1 lb	fresh asparagus	500 g
¾ cup	mayonnaise	175 mL
¼ cup	milk	50 mL
2 tbsp	finely chopped onion	25 mL
1 tbsp	lemon juice	15 mL
¼ tsp	EACH: salt, pepper	1 mL
⅛ tsp	EACH: cayenne pepper, garlic powder	0.5 mL
1	can (7 oz / 198 g) flaked tuna, drained	1
4	hard-cooked eggs, diced	4

In a small saucepan, sprinkle gelatine over cold water. Place over low heat; stir constantly until gelatine is completely dissolved. Remove from heat. Cook asparagus until tender-crisp; drain and chop into ¼-inch (6 mm) pieces. In a large bowl, combine mayonnaise, milk, onion, lemon juice and seasonings. Stir gelatine into salad dressing mixture. Fold asparagus, tuna and eggs into mixture. Turn into a lightly oiled 4-cup (1 L) mold. Chill 2 hours until set. Unmold and garnish with asparagus tips for the crowning finish.

Makes 6 servings.

Calories per serving: 340   Vitamin C: Excellent   Vitamin A: Good

ENSALADA DE NOCHE BUENA

Preparation: about 10 minutes

In Mexico, Christmas Eve Salad served with Chicken or Turkey Mole (page 73) is part of the Christmas Eve tradition. However, it is so good that it deserves to be served throughout the year.

1	head lettuce, shredded	1
3	oranges, peeled and sectioned	3
2	firm bananas, sliced crosswise	2
1	large unpeeled apple, cored and diced	1
1 cup	pineapple chunks, fresh or canned	250 mL
1 cup	sliced canned beets	250 mL
½ cup	coarsely chopped toasted peanuts	125 mL
¼ cup	whole cranberry sauce	50 mL
	or	
	Seeds of 1 pomegranate	

On a platter, make a bed of lettuce; arrange fruit and beets over it; top with peanuts and cranberry sauce. Serve with either Vinaigrette Dressing (page 39) or Creamy Mexican Dressing (page 37).

Makes approximately 8–10 servings.

TIP: Dip banana and apple sections in lemon juice before assembling salad to prevent the fruit from turning brown.

Calories per serving: 160   Fiber and vitamin C: Excellent

TEN-MINUTE TACO SALAD

Preparation: about 15 minutes   Cook: about 15 minutes

All the ingredients of a deluxe taco are included in this popular Mexican salad. Serve it for a main course with Sober Sangria (page 148) and fresh fruit.

1 lb	ground beef	500 g
1	package MexiCasa Taco Seasoning Mix	1
¾ cup	water	175 mL
1	can (14 oz/398 mL) red kidney beans, undrained	1
4	tomatoes, cut in wedges	4
1	avocado, peeled and cut in thin slices	1
½	package MexiCasa Nacho Chips	½
1	head lettuce, torn in small pieces	1
2 cups	grated Black Diamond Cheddar Cheese	500 mL
1 cup	chopped mild onion	250 mL
¾ cup	MexiCasa Taco Relish *or* Mexican Salad Dressing (recipe follows)	175 mL

In a skillet, brown ground beef; drain fat. Add seasoning mix, water and beans. Bring to a boil, then reduce heat, cover and simmer 10 minutes until moist but not runny. Reserve some tomato wedges, avocado slices and nacho chips for use as a garnish. In a large salad bowl, combine all remaining ingredients; add hot ground beef mixture and lightly toss, or serve hot meat alongside the cold salad rather than tossed. Garnish with reserved tomato, avocado and nachos.

Makes 6–8 servings.

TIP: This salad can be made ahead: cut up all the vegetables and grate the cheese. At serving time, reheat the meat and toss the salad, but remember that it is best served immediately.

Calories per serving: 483   Fiber; vitamins A and C; calcium; iron: Excellent

---

MEXICAN SALAD DRESSING   Preparation: under 5 minutes

½ cup	MexiCasa Taco Relish	125 mL
⅓ cup	mayonnaise	75 mL

In a small bowl, combine all ingredients. Chill until ready to use. Serve over salad greens or as a relish or dip.

Makes about ¾ cup (175 mL).

CARTWHEEL SALAD

Preparation: about 10 minutes   Chill: about 1 hour

Each of the ingredients in this special salad are arranged in wedge shapes like those formed by the spokes of a wheel.

1	small head iceberg lettuce torn in bite-size pieces	1
1	small head romaine lettuce, torn in bite-size pieces	1
1 cup	cherry tomato halves *or* chopped tomato	250 mL
½ cup	chick-peas, drained	125 mL
½ cup	chopped beets	125 mL
¼ cup	grated carrot *or* sliced ripe olives	50 mL
¼ cup	sliced radishes	50 mL
¼ cup	sliced green onion	50 mL
	MexiCasa Nacho Chips	

Prepare all ingredients and chill. In a large shallow salad bowl, make a bed of lettuce and arrange vegetables in a cartwheel design. To serve, drizzle with Creamy Mexican Dressing (page 37) and garnish with nacho chips.

Makes 6–8 servings.

Calories per serving: 154   Fiber; vitamins A and C: Good   Iron: Good

PASTA-BEAN SALAD

Preparation: about 15 minutes   Chill: 2 hours

If you're looking for an unusual salad, try this recipe; it's a unique combination of contrasting textures and colors.

2 cups	cooked, drained shell pasta	500 mL
1	can (14 oz/398 mL) red kidney beans, rinsed and drained	1
1 cup	frozen broccoli florets, thawed and drained	250 mL
1 cup	EACH: diced carrots, sliced celery	250 mL
¾ cup	mayonnaise	175 mL
¼ cup	chopped fresh parsley	50 mL
¼ cup	Black Diamond Grated Parmesan Cheese	50 mL
2 tbsp	lemon juice	25 mL
1	clove garlic, minced	1
1 tsp	dried basil	5 mL
	Lettuce leaves (optional)	

In a large bowl, combine pasta, beans, broccoli, carrots and celery; toss gently. Combine mayonnaise, parsley, cheese, lemon juice, garlic and basil; add to macaroni mixture, tossing gently to coat. Cover and chill 2 hours. Serve on lettuce leaves, if desired.

Makes 4 servings.

Calories per serving: 545   Fiber; vitamins A and C: Excellent   Calcium and iron: Good

TABBOULEH

Preparation: about 15 minutes   Cook: 5 minutes   Chill: 2–3 hours or overnight

Mint is a favorite herb of mine that I grow in the garden. I enjoy using it in this Middle Eastern salad, which can be made well ahead of time.

½ cup	uncooked long-grain brown rice	125 mL
¾ cup	boiling water	175 mL
2	large bunches parsley, chopped	2
1	bunch green onions, chopped	1
1½ cups	diced tomatoes	375 mL
¼ cup	fresh mint *or* 1 tbsp (15 mL) dried mint	50 mL
	Juice of 1 lemon	
1 cup	Lemon Garlic Dressing (page 38)	250 mL

Cook rice in boiling water, covered, for 5 minutes; drain. In a large salad bowl, combine all ingredients and chill 2–3 hours or overnight before serving.

Makes 10 servings.

TIP: Store parsley, watercress and mint in tightly covered jars or containers.

Calories per serving: 180   Vitamins A and C: Excellent

CANTONESE FISH AND PASTA SALAD

Preparation: about 20 minutes   Cook: 10 minutes   Chill: 30 minutes

This salad is at its best prepared ahead of time. When you're ready to serve it, just fold in the chunks of fish fillets.

8 cups	water	2 L
⅓ cup	melted Becel Margarine, divided	75 mL
1½ cups	uncooked macaroni	375 mL
3 tbsp	soy sauce	45 mL
1 tbsp	dry sherry	15 mL
2 tbsp	cider vinegar	25 mL
¼ tsp	EACH: ground ginger, garlic powder	1 mL
¼ tsp	freshly ground black pepper	1 mL
2 cups	snow peas, trimmed and halved	500 mL
1 cup	sliced celery	250 mL
1 cup	red *or* green pepper, cut in matchsticks	250 mL
½ lb	cooked fish fillets, cut in chunks	250 g
1 tbsp	toasted sesame seeds	15 mL

In a large saucepan, bring water and 2 tbsp (25 mL) margarine to a boil. Add macaroni. Cook, stirring occasionally, until just tender, about 10 minutes. Drain and set aside. In a large bowl, combine soy sauce, sherry, vinegar, ginger, garlic powder, pepper and remaining margarine; mix well. Add peas, celery, red or green pepper and macaroni; toss to coat. Cover and chill at least 30 minutes. Just before serving, fold in fish. Sprinkle with sesame seeds.

Makes 6 servings.

TIP: To toast sesame seeds, cook and stir in a small skillet over medium heat until golden, about 3 minutes.

Calories per serving: 295   Vitamin C: Excellent   Fiber, vitamin A and iron: Good

PACK 'N TOTE CHEF'S SALAD

Preparation: 20 minutes   Chill: 8 hours or overnight

This is the best "pack and tote" salad I know. One of my cottage friends, who is an avid fisherman, calls this recipe a "keeper."

1 cup	**Creamy Caesar Dressing** (see below)	250 mL
4 cups	**sliced fresh mushrooms**	1 L
1 cup	**chopped celery**	250 mL
1	**tomato, chopped**	1
½	**medium cucumber, sliced**	½
1	**small red onion, sliced and separated into rings**	1
1 cup	**grated Black Diamond Cheddar Cheese** *or* **Swiss cheese**	250 mL
1	**hard-cooked egg, chopped**	1

Prepare dressing. In a large salad bowl, layer all ingredients in order given. Spread prepared dressing over top, cover and chill for at least 8 hours or overnight.

Makes 5–6 servings.

Calories per serving: 284 Calcium: Excellent   Vitamins A and C: Good

SALAD DRESSINGS

All of the following homemade dressings are easy to prepare and have a refreshing taste. Make up three or four varieties and keep them in the refrigerator — they can be stored for several weeks.

CREAMY CAESAR DRESSING

Preparation: about 5 minutes   Chill: about 30 minutes

This dressing is perfect with Pack 'N Tote Chef's Salad (see above).

1	**package WishBone Classic Caesar Dressing**	1
2 tbsp	**water**	25 mL
¼ cup	**cider vinegar**	50 mL
1	**egg**	1
⅔ cup	**dairy sour cream**	150 mL
2 tsp	**prepared mustard**	10 mL

In a small bowl, blend dressing with water. Add vinegar and egg and beat thoroughly. Add sour cream and mustard; blend well. Chill about 30 minutes before serving.

Makes approximately 1 cup (250 mL).

TIP: Greens and other vegetables must be free of moisture so the dressings will cling.

Calories per 1 tbsp (15 mL): 26 Low fat

CREAMY MEXICAN DRESSING

Preparation: about 5 minutes   Chill: 1–2 hours or overnight

Buttermilk combined with herbs gives a subtle taste to this dressing. Use it with Cartwheel Salad (page 34) or your favorite tossed green salad.

¾ cup	dairy sour cream	175 mL	In a container that can be tightly sealed, combine all ingredients. Shake well. Chill 1–2 hours or overnight for best flavor.
⅓ cup	EACH: mayonnaise, buttermilk	75 mL	
1 tbsp	EACH: lemon juice, water	15 mL	**Makes about 1½ cups (375 mL).**
½ tsp	Lawry's Seasoned Salt	2 mL	
¼ tsp	EACH: garlic powder, oregano	1 mL	
¼ tsp	EACH: basil, dry mustard, Lawry's Seasoned Pepper	1 mL	
3 tbsp	minced parsley	45 mL	

Calories per 1 tbsp (15 mL): 32

COUNTRY-STYLE DRESSING

Preparation: about 5 minutes   Chill: about 30 minutes

The creaminess of this dressing makes it a natural for spinach salads.

¾ cup	dairy sour cream *or* yogurt	175 mL	In a small bowl, combine all ingredients with a whisk or a fork; blend thoroughly. Chill about 30 minutes before serving.
⅓ cup	EACH: mayonnaise, buttermilk	75 mL	
1 tbsp	EACH: lemon juice, water	15 mL	**Makes approximately 1½ cups (375 mL).**
½ tsp	Lawry's Seasoned Salt	2 mL	
⅛ tsp	EACH: garlic powder, oregano	0.5 mL	TIP: Many salad dressing flavors improve if made ahead and chilled several hours before serving.
¼ tsp	EACH: basil, dry mustard	1 mL	
¼ tsp	Lawry's Seasoned Pepper	1 mL	

Calories per 1 tbsp (15 mL): 32

HONEY LIME FRUIT DRESSING

Preparation: about 5 minutes

You'll want to serve this dressing over luscious fresh summer fruits such as berries, melons, peaches, nectarines and green grapes.

⅓ cup	EACH: lime juice, salad oil	75 mL	In a container that can be tightly sealed, combine all ingredients. Shake well.
½ tsp	grated lime peel	2 mL	
2 tbsp	honey	25 mL	**Makes approximately ¾ cup (175 mL).**

Calories per 1 tbsp (15 mL): 77

LEMON GARLIC DRESSING

Preparation: about 5 minutes   Chill: 1–2 hours

This dressing is perfect for a simple fruit salad or an unusual salad like Tabbouleh (page 35). When a creamy but lower calorie version is desired, use buttermilk to replace vegetable oil.

3 tbsp	EACH: lemon juice, water	45 mL	
1 tbsp	finely minced parsley	15 mL	
1/2 tsp	EACH: grated lemon peel, dry mustard, sugar, Lawry's Seasoned Salt	2 mL	
1	small clove garlic, minced	1	
1/4 tsp	turmeric	1 mL	
Dash	Lawry's Seasoned Pepper	Dash	
2/3 cup	vegetable oil *or* buttermilk	150 mL	

In a container that can be tightly sealed, combine all ingredients except oil. Shake well. Add oil and shake again for 30 seconds. For best flavor, chill 1–2 hours before serving.

Makes approximately 1 cup (250 mL).

Calories per 1 tbsp (15 mL): 78

YOLK-FREE MAYONNAISE

Preparation: about 5 minutes

You'll look a long time before you find a recipe for Yolk-Free Mayonnaise. This recipe has been developed for people who are watching their cholesterol intake.

1	egg white	1
1 tbsp	vinegar	15 mL
1 tsp	sugar	5 mL
1/2 tsp	dry mustard	2 mL
Dash	pepper	Dash
1/2 cup	melted Becel Margarine, cooled	125 mL

In a blender or food processor, blend egg white, vinegar, sugar, mustard and pepper on high for 30 seconds. With the motor running, slowly add the melted margarine; blend until thick and creamy. Refrigerate until ready to use.

Makes 1/2 cup (125 mL).

TIP: When making mayonnaise, be sure all the ingredients are at room temperature. This one can be doubled and refrigerated for future use.

Calories per 1 tbsp (15 mL): 110

OLD-FASHIONED COOKED SALAD DRESSING

Preparation: about 5 minutes   Cook: about 5 minutes

Our mothers made this style of dressing before commercial dressings became available. Try it again as a change-of-flavor. It's also in keeping with today's interest in lowering cholesterol in our diets.

1 tsp	dry mustard	5 mL
1–2 tbsp	sugar	15–25 mL
½ tsp	salt	2 mL
2 tbsp	all-purpose flour	25 mL
¼ tsp	paprika (optional)	1 mL
¾ cup	cold water	175 mL
¼ cup	vinegar	50 mL
2 tbsp	Becel Margarine	25 mL

In a medium saucepan, combine all ingredients except margarine. Cook over medium-low heat, stirring constantly, until smooth and thickened, about 5 minutes. Add margarine, stir to melt. Cool and store in refrigerator.

Microwave: In a 2-cup (500 mL) measure, combine dry ingredients. Stir in water and vinegar, heat at HIGH (100%) 3–5 minutes; stir every minute until thickened. Add margarine, stir to melt. Cool slightly; refrigerate.

Makes 1 cup (250 mL).

TIP: Try this dressing with potato salad and seafood salads.

Calories per 1 tbsp (15 mL): 18

VINAIGRETTE DRESSING

Preparation: about 5 minutes   Chill: 1-2 hours

Ready in an instant, this dressing is always popular because of its unlimited variations and affinity for most salads. The French dress their salads with it and serve them after the main course to cleanse the palate.

¼ cup	red wine vinegar	50 mL
1 tbsp	EACH: water, lemon juice	15 mL
1 tsp	sugar	5 mL
½ tsp	EACH: basil, Lawry's Seasoned Salt and Seasoned Pepper	2 mL
1	clove garlic, minced	1
¼ tsp	EACH: paprika, dry mustard, tarragon, celery seed	1 mL
⅔ cup	salad oil	150 mL

In a container that can be tightly sealed, combine vinegar, water, lemon juice, sugar and seasonings. Blend or shake well. Add oil; blend or shake again. For best flavor, chill 1–2 hours before serving.

Makes approximately 1 cup (250 mL).

TIPS: 1. Red wine is superior to malt and cider in this recipe. 2. Oil and vinegar dressings separate on standing. Shake vigorously before serving to make sure all ingredients are well mixed.

Calories per 1 tbsp (15 mL): 79

VARIATION

Confetti Dressing: Add chopped green pepper, pimiento or red pepper, hard-cooked eggs and pickled beets to Vinaigrette Dressing. Great on tossed greens or as a marinade for blanched vegetables.

EGGS AND CHEESE

Eggs and cheese are two foods that always make short work of meal preparation and are good for you, too. Both are important sources of protein. As well, cheese is a valuable source of calcium. Calcium's importance in the diet is more widely recognized today; a serving of only 1½ ounces (42 g) of cheese provides the recommended daily requirement of calcium for adults.

QUICK SEASONING TIPS

Herbs frequently used with eggs and cheese are: basil, cayenne pepper, celery seed, dill, curry, marjoram, oregano, parsley, tarragon and thyme. For more unusual flavors, use caraway seeds, chili powder, sage and cumin. Before using dried herbs, crush them in the palm of your hand to release all of their flavor. Because herbs lose strength with age, buy them in small quantities and store in tightly closed jars away from heat, light and moisture.

CREATIVE GARNISHING TIPS

Eggs and cheese dishes are naturals for garnishes. Use a cluster of spinach leaves with cherry tomatoes and chopped cooked egg white for the Florentine Cheese Soufflé (page 42). Cut cheese slices in half and overlap a few triangles on top of the Cheesy Macaroni and Vegetables (page 48) or simply use grated cheese on overlapping tomato slices. For Onion Mushroom Lazy Day Bake (page 44) use a lazy garnish by topping with rings of red and green peppers. Scatter sliced mushrooms and snipped fresh parsley on the Healthy Heart Omelette (page 45). These dishes are simple but lovely, because they contrast so well with the bright garnishes.

SPICY DEVILED EGG CASSEROLE

Preparation: about 15 minutes   Cook: about 30 minutes

Popular deviled eggs taste even better in this economical prepared-ahead oven dish.

6	hard-cooked eggs, peeled	6
½ cup	cottage cheese	125 mL
2 tbsp	mayonnaise	25 mL
½ cup	finely diced celery	125 mL
¼ cup	finely diced onion	50 mL
1 tbsp	margarine *or* butter	15 mL
½ tsp	curry powder	2 mL
2 cups	milk	500 mL
1	pouch Lipton Bon Appétit Chicken Noodle Supreme Soup	1
1 tbsp	chopped fresh parsley	15 mL
½ tsp	paprika	2 mL

Cut eggs in half lengthwise; remove yolks. In a small bowl, combine yolks with cottage cheese, mayonnaise and celery. Fill egg whites with yolk mixture. In a medium saucepan, cook onions in margarine until transparent; blend in curry powder. Add milk and stir in soup mix. Bring to a boil, then reduce heat, cover and simmer 7 minutes. Place 1 cup (250 mL) sauce in a greased 11 × 7-inch (2 L) baking dish; arrange eggs on sauce. Pour remaining sauce over top. Sprinkle with parsley and paprika. Bake at 350°F (180°C) 25–30 minutes or until bubbly.

Microwave: Prepare yolk filling and fill whites as above. In a 6-cup (1.5 L) covered casserole, melt margarine at HIGH (100%) 45 seconds. Add onions and heat at HIGH 2–3 minutes; stir in curry powder, milk and soup mix. Heat at HIGH 4–5 minutes; stir once. Assemble as above; heat at HIGH 8–10 minutes or until bubbly. Let stand, covered, 5 minutes.

Makes 4–6 servings.

Calories per serving: 225   Calcium and vitamin A: Good

FLORENTINE CHEESE SOUFFLÉ

Preparation: about 15 minutes   Cook: 1 hour

Glamorous soufflés are considered difficult, yet really are easy. This soufflé uses shortcuts in the preparation — Lipton Cheddar Cheese Soup and frozen spinach.

1	pouch Lipton Cheddar Cheese Soup	1
2 tbsp	all-purpose flour	25 mL
1 cup	milk	250 mL
1 tbsp	chopped onion	15 mL
1/2 tsp	nutmeg	2 mL
1	package (300 g) frozen chopped spinach, cooked and well drained	1
4	eggs, separated	4
¼ tsp	cream of tartar	1 mL

In a medium saucepan, combine soup mix, flour, milk, onion and nutmeg. Cook, stirring constantly, over medium heat, about 5 minutes or until thickened. Add well-drained spinach. In a small bowl, beat egg yolks at high speed until thick and lemon-colored. Blend a small amount of hot soup mixture into yolks, then return to soup mixture. In a large bowl, beat egg whites and cream of tartar at high speed until stiff but not dry. Gently but thoroughly fold soup-yolk mixture into whites. Carefully pour into a greased 10-cup (2.5 L) soufflé dish. Bake at 350°F (180°C) 55–60 minutes or until golden brown. Serve immediately. Soufflés do not wait for latecomers.

Makes 6 servings.

TIPS: 1. Always bake soufflés in the center of a preheated oven. 2. Don't peek until 5 minutes before end of baking time or soufflé may fall.

Calories per serving: 125   Vitamin A: Excellent   Fiber and calcium: Good

Clockwise: Cartwheel Salad (page 34); Fresh Citrus Pasta Salad (page 31); Creamy Mexican Dressing (page 37)

VERSATILE CHEESE STRATA

Preparation: about 15 minutes   Chill: 4–5 hours or overnight   Cook: 35 minutes

This terrific recipe is best made the night before and then popped into the oven about half an hour before serving for a brunch or a light supper.

6	slices whole wheat *or* white bread, crusts removed	6
3 cups	grated Black Diamond Cheddar Cheese *or* Mozzarella Cheese	750 mL
6	eggs, beaten	6
2 cups	milk	500 mL
1	green onion, diced	1
1 tsp	Lawry's Seasoned Salt	5 mL
1	tomato, cut into wedges	1

Arrange bread slices in bottom of a lightly greased 13 × 9-inch (3.5 L) baking dish. Sprinkle with half the cheese. In a medium bowl, blend eggs, milk, onion and salt; pour over bread. Sprinkle with remaining cheese. Cover with plastic wrap, refrigerate for several hours or overnight. Top with tomato wedges; bake, uncovered, at 350°F (180°C) 35 minutes or until light golden brown. Let stand 5 minutes.

Makes 6 servings.

Calories per serving: 443   Calcium and vitamin A: Excellent   Riboflavin and iron: Good

VARIATIONS

Broccoli Cheese Strata: Arrange 1 package (300g) frozen, chopped broccoli, cooked and drained, over bread slices; top with cheese. Pour milk-egg mixture over bread. Bake as above.
Mexican Cheese Strata: Pour 1 bottle (250 mL) MexiCasa Taco Relish over Strata 5 minutes before end of baking time.

Mushroom Cheese Strata: Saute ½ lb (250 g) sliced fresh mushrooms in 2 tbsp (25 mL) margarine *or* butter. Add to egg mixture and continue with directions for Strata.

TIP: Combine two cheeses for a more interesting flavor.

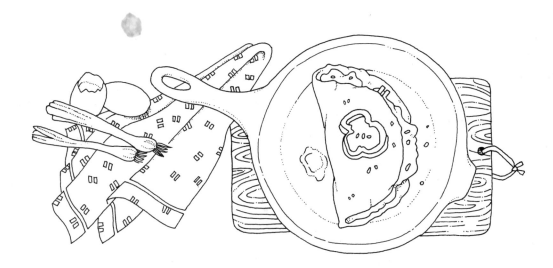

Clockwise: Ham and Cheese Frittata (page 47); New Orleans Cajun-Style Eggs (page 49)

ONION MUSHROOM LAZY DAY BAKE

Preparation: about 10 minutes   Cook: 30 minutes

My teenage daughter loves preparing this quiche for supper. Because she doesn't have to make a pastry base, it is prepared in minutes.

1	pouch Lipton Onion-Mushroom Soup	1
3	eggs, slightly beaten	3
1½ cups	milk	375 mL
½ cup	finely crushed unsalted soda crackers	125 mL
½ tsp	dry mustard	2 mL
½ cup	EACH: grated Black Diamond Old Cheddar Cheese, chopped ham	125 mL
1	tomato, finely diced	1
3	green pepper rings	3

In a medium bowl, blend soup mix, eggs, milk, crackers, mustard, cheese and ham. Pour into a lightly greased 9-inch (23 cm) pie plate. Top with tomato and green pepper. Bake at 350°F (180°C) 30–40 minutes or until just set. Cut into wedges to serve.

Microwave: Assemble as above. Sprinkle with paprika if desired. Cover with waxed paper. Heat at MEDIUM (50%) 14–16 minutes or until knife inserted in middle comes out clean. Rotate dish once during cooking. Let stand, covered, 5 minutes.

Makes 5–6 servings.

Calories per serving: 191   Vitamin C: Excellent   Calcium and vitamin A: Good

VARIATION

Mexican Bake: Add 1–2 tbsp (15–25 mL) chopped MexiCasa Jalapeño Peppers.

INDIVIDUAL QUICHE MEXICANA

Preparation: about 10 minutes   Cook: 25 minutes

This novel combination of Mexican and French cuisines uses softened corn tostada shells to replace pastry for easily prepared individual servings of quiche.

1	package MexiCasa Tostada Shells (10)	1
1 cup	grated Black Diamond Mozzarella Cheese	250 mL
3	eggs, well beaten	3
¼ cup	light cream	50 mL
2 tbsp	finely chopped onion	25 mL
¼ cup	chopped green pepper	50 mL
2 tbsp	diced pimiento	25 mL
¼ tsp	EACH: Lawry's Seasoned Salt, Garlic Powder, Seasoned Pepper	1 mL

Soften tostada shells by dipping in warm water for 30 seconds; wrap moist shells tightly in foil; steam bake for 5 minutes at 350°F (180°C). Separate softened shells and fit into small cus-tard cups or a muffin tin to form tortilla quiche-cups. In a medium bowl, thoroughly combine remaining ingredients. Pour about ¼ cup (50 mL) egg mixture into each quiche-cup. Bake at 325°F (160°C) 15–20 minutes.

Microwave: Soften tostada shells by dipping in warm water for 30 seconds; do not shake off excess water. Place wet shells in plastic bag, add 1 tbsp (15 mL) water; wrap securely. Heat at HIGH (100%) for 1–1½ minutes. Form tortilla quiche-cups; prepare egg mixture and fill as directed above. Heat at HIGH 4–5 minutes. Let stand 3–5 minutes.

Makes 10 individual quiches.

TIP: Brushing the cheese grater with vegetable oil will make it easier to clean after use.

Calories per quiche: 183   Calcium: Good

OMELETTE WITH PIZAZZ

Preparation: about 5 minutes   Cook: about 5 minutes

When you want to give an omelette extra pizazz, go Italian by adding tomatoes, pepperoni, oregano and basil.

6	eggs	6
¼ cup	water	50 mL
½ tsp	salt	2 mL
2 tbsp	margarine *or* butter	25 mL
1 tsp	EACH: oregano, basil	5 mL
¼ cup	ketchup	50 mL
12	thin slices pepperoni *or* salami	12
2	tomatoes, thinly sliced	2
½ cup	sliced fresh mushrooms	125 mL
1 cup	grated Black Diamond Mozzarella Cheese	250 mL

In a small bowl, blend eggs, water and salt. In a large skillet, over medium-high heat, melt margarine. Sprinkle oregano and basil in pan; add egg mixture. Lift set edges of omelette, tilting pan to allow uncooked egg to flow to the bottom. When omelette is almost set but surface is still moist, top with ketchup, pepperoni, tomatoes, mushrooms and cheese. Cover, leave on low heat until cheese melts, about 30 seconds. Slice into 3 triangles.

Microwave: Prepare egg mixture as above. In a medium casserole, melt margarine at HIGH (100%) 1 minute; add egg mixture and heat, covered, at MEDIUM (50%) 3–4 minutes; stir occasionally. Top with ketchup, pepperoni, tomatoes, mushrooms and cheese. Heat, covered, 1½ minutes. Let stand, covered, 2 minutes or until set.

Makes 2–3 servings.

Calories per serving: 644   Calcium, vitamins A and C: Excellent   Iron and protein: Good

HEALTHY HEART OMELETTE

Preparation: about 10 minutes   Cook: about 5 minutes per omelette

This yolkless omelette gets good health reviews because it's low in cholesterol and sodium.

¼ cup	Becel Margarine, divided	50 mL
1 cup	sliced fresh mushrooms	250 mL
½ cup	onion rings	125 mL
⅔ cup	cherry tomato halves	150 mL
8	egg whites	8
2 tbsp	non-fat dry milk powder	25 mL
⅛ tsp	freshly ground black pepper	0.5 mL
¼ tsp	paprika	1 mL
	Chopped fresh parsley	

In a medium skillet, over medium-high heat, melt 1 tbsp (15 mL) margarine. Sauté mushrooms and onion until onion is transparent, about 4 minutes. Add tomatoes and sauté for 1 minute; remove from pan; cover to keep warm. In a small bowl, beat egg whites, milk powder, pepper, paprika and 2 tbsp (25 mL) melted margarine, until foamy. In the same skillet, melt remaining margarine. Add half the egg mixture. Cook over low heat until the bottom of the omelette is set. Lift set edges of omelette, tilting pan to allow uncooked egg to flow to the bottom. Cook until omelette is almost set but surface is still moist. Fill with reserved vegetable mixture. Fold omelette in half on a serving plate; cover and keep warm. Repeat for second omelette. Sprinkle with chopped parsley before serving.

Microwave: In a 9-inch (23 cm) pie plate, melt 1 tbsp (15 mL) margarine; add mushrooms and onion. Heat at HIGH (100%) 2–3 minutes; stir once. Add tomatoes and heat at HIGH 1–1½ minutes. Set aside, covered to keep warm. Prepare egg mixture as above. Melt remaining margarine in pie plate; add half the egg mixture. Heat at MEDIUM (50%) 3–4 minutes until set. Fill as directed above. Repeat for second omelette.

Makes 2 servings.

Calories per omelette: 285   Vitamin A: Excellent

SPEEDY SKILLET SUPPER

Preparation: about 10 minutes   Cook: about 5 minutes

Eggs are one of Nature's true convenience foods. If you have only ten minutes to prepare dinner, remember this recipe.

2 tbsp	margarine *or* butter	25 mL
½ cup	EACH: chopped onion, green pepper	125 mL
8	eggs	8
¼ cup	milk	50 mL
1 tsp	Lawry's Seasoned Salt	5 mL
½ tsp	crushed basil	2 mL
¼ tsp	Lawry's Seasoned Pepper	1 mL
1	package (125 g) cream cheese, cubed	1
1	medium tomato, chopped	1
2–4	slices bacon, cooked and crumbled	2–4

In a large skillet, over medium-high heat, melt margarine. Sauté onion and green pepper until tender. In a small bowl, blend eggs, milk and seasonings. Pour egg mixture over onion and green pepper; add cream cheese and tomato. Cook over low heat until eggs are thickened but still moist. Fold in half on a serving plate. Garnish with bacon and serve.

Microwave: In an 8-cup (2 L) covered casserole, melt margarine at HIGH (100%) 1 minute. Add onion and green pepper; heat, covered, at HIGH 3 minutes. Prepare egg mixture; pour into casserole; add cream cheese and tomato. Heat at HIGH 3 minutes; stir. Heat at MEDIUM (50%) 5–7 minutes; rotate dish once. Garnish with bacon. Let stand, covered, 5 minutes.

Makes 4 servings.

Calories per serving: 360   Vitamins A and C: Excellent   Iron and riboflavin: Good

CHILI CHEESE JUBILEE

Preparation: about 10 minutes   Cook: about 30 minutes

If ever there was an oven-to-table dish, this is it. Use a Pyrex casserole so your guests can enjoy the layers of colorful ingredients.

1	medium onion, chopped	1
½ cup	diced green pepper	125 mL
2 tbsp	margarine *or* butter	25 mL
1	can (7½ oz/213 mL) tomato sauce	1
1	package MexiCasa Chili Seasoning Mix	1
½ cup	water	125 mL
2	eggs, slightly beaten	2
1 cup	light cream	250 mL
½	package MexiCasa Nacho Chips, divided	½
4½ cups	grated Black Diamond Mild Cheddar *or* Colby Cheese, divided	1.1 L
1 cup	dairy sour cream	250 mL

In a medium skillet, over medium-high heat, sauté onion and green pepper in margarine; add tomato sauce, seasoning mix and water. Simmer, uncovered, 5 minutes. Remove from heat. Combine eggs and cream. Add slowly, stirring constantly. In a greased 8-cup (2 L) casserole, place half nacho chips. Add 2 cups (500 mL) cheese and half sauce. Repeat layers once. Bake, uncovered, at 325°F (160°C) 25–30 minutes. Top with sour cream and remaining cheese during last 10 minutes. Let stand 10 minutes before cutting into squares.

Microwave: In an 8-cup (2 L) casserole, melt margarine at HIGH (100%) 45 seconds. Add onion and green pepper; heat at HIGH 3 minutes; stir occasionally. Add tomato sauce, chili seasoning mix and water. Heat at HIGH 2–3 minutes; combine eggs and cream and add slowly. Assemble as above. Heat at HIGH 8–10 minutes. Top with sour cream and remaining cheese; heat at HIGH 2 minutes. Let stand 5 minutes.

Makes 7–8 servings.

TIPS: 1. Casserole may be frozen, without sour cream and cheese topping. 2. Coat casserole dish with vegetable oil spray for easier serving and cleaning.

Calories per serving: 793   Calcium and vitamin A: Excellent   Iron and vitamin C: Good

HAM AND CHEESE FRITTATA CASSEROLE

Preparation: about 10 minutes   Cook: about 15 minutes

Treat your family to this easy version of an Italian omelette. It's a meal in itself.

2 tbsp	margarine *or* butter	25 mL
1½ cups	frozen hash brown potatoes	375 mL
1	small carrot, grated	1
2	green onions, chopped	2
¼ cup	chopped celery	50 mL
8	eggs	8
½ cup	milk	125 mL
¼ tsp	EACH: dry mustard, pepper	1 mL
1	can (6 ½ oz/184 g) Puritan Flaked Ham	1
¾ cup	grated Black Diamond Cheddar Cheese	175 mL

In a medium skillet, over medium-high heat, melt margarine. Add potatoes, carrot, onion and celery; cook about 8 minutes. In a small bowl, combine eggs, milk and spices. Pour over cooked vegetable mixture. Separate ham, sprinkle on top; cook over medium heat, lifting the edges to allow uncooked egg to run to the bottom. Cook until just set, but still moist on the surface, about 5–7 minutes. Sprinkle with cheese, cover and reduce to low heat until cheese melts, about 30 seconds. Cut into wedges to serve.

Microwave: In an 8-cup (2 L) covered casserole, combine margarine, potatoes, carrot, onion and celery. Heat at HIGH (100%) 5–7 minutes; stir once. Combine eggs, milk and spices; pour over vegetables; sprinkle with ham. Heat, covered, at HIGH 3 minutes; stir. Heat at MEDIUM (50%) 8–10 minutes; rotate dish once. Sprinkle with cheese; heat, covered, at HIGH 45–60 seconds until cheese melts. Let stand, covered, 5 minutes.

Makes 4–6 servings.

Calories per serving: 457   Iron and vitamin A: Excellent   Calcium and vitamin C: Good

EGG-FILLED TACOS

Preparation: about 10 minutes   Cook: about 5 minutes

Eggs are an important part of Mexican cuisine. Try these Egg-Filled Tacos for a novel breakfast treat.

6	eggs	6
Dash	salt and pepper	Dash
½ cup	water *or* milk	125 mL
1	small onion, coarsely chopped	1
1 tbsp	margarine *or* butter	15 mL
½ cup	grated Black Diamond Cheddar *or* Mozzarella Cheese	125 mL
1	package MexiCasa Taco Shells (10)	1
	Bacon bits, MexiCasa Taco Relish, sautéed mushrooms	

In a small bowl, combine eggs, salt, pepper and liquid. In a skillet, sauté onion in margarine. Add egg mixture to onion; cook over moderate heat, stirring occasionally. Add cheese just before eggs are set. Heat taco shells according to package directions. Spoon egg mixture into warm taco shells and top with bacon bits, taco relish and/or sautéed mushrooms.

Makes 5–6 tacos.

Calories per taco: 259, without toppings   Calcium: Good

CHEESY MACARONI AND VEGETABLES

Preparation: about 10 minutes   Cook: about 35 minutes

Convenience foods make short work of meal preparation. In this recipe, Lipton Minestrone Soup provides a different flavor and texture to macaroni and cheese.

¾ cup	uncooked macaroni	175 mL
2 cups	water	500 mL
1	pouch Lipton Bon Appétit Minestrone Soup	1
1½ cups	grated Black Diamond Mozzarella *or* Cheddar Cheese, divided	375 mL
1 tbsp	margarine *or* butter	15 mL
½ cup	milk	125 mL
½ cup	coarse bread crumbs	125 mL

In a medium saucepan, combine macaroni, water and soup mix. Cook, covered, 10–12 minutes. Add 1 cup (250 mL) cheese, margarine and milk. Place in a greased casserole; top with crumbs and remaining cheese. Bake at 350°F (180°C) 25–30 minutes until crumbs are browned.

Microwave: In an 8-cup (2 L) casserole, combine macaroni, water and soup mix. Heat at HIGH (100%) 3 minutes; heat at MEDIUM (50%) 10–12 minutes; stir once or twice. Add 1 cup (250 mL) cheese, margarine and milk; top with crumbs, remaining cheese; sprinkle with paprika if desired. Heat at HIGH 4½–6 minutes or until heated through. Rotate dish after 3 minutes.

Makes 3–4 servings.

Calories per serving: 500   Calcium: Excellent   Vitamin A: Good

VARIATION

Harvest Macaroni: Add diced cooked ham, cooked bacon pieces or diced cooked sausage to macaroni before baking.

HUEVOS RANCHEROS

Preparation: about 5 minutes   Cook: about 15 minutes

This is a Mexican classic. When you taste it, you'll know why! Serve it with rice and a green salad.

1	clove garlic, minced	1
1	medium onion, chopped	1
¼ cup	chopped green pepper	50 mL
1 tbsp	Imperial Margarine	15 mL
1	can (14 oz/398 mL) tomatoes, undrained and chopped	1
1 tsp	chili powder	5 mL
½ tsp	EACH: oregano, salt	2 mL
¼ tsp	cumin (optional)	1 mL
⅛ tsp	pepper	0.5 mL
6	eggs	6
1	package MexiCasa Tostada Shells (10)	1

In a large skillet, sauté garlic, onion and green pepper in margarine until softened, about 2–3 minutes. Add tomatoes, chili powder, oregano, salt, cumin and pepper. Simmer and stir occasionally for 10 minutes to blend flavors. Break eggs into sauce; cover skillet; cook slowly over medium heat until eggs are set, about 6–8 minutes. Warm 6 tostada shells according to package directions. Serve eggs with sauce on warm tostada shells.

Makes 6 servings.

TIP: Use remaining tostada shells for mini-pizzas; top with tomato sauce, cheese and your favorite pizza garnishes.

Calories per serving: 225   Vitamin C: Excellent   Vitamin A and iron: Good

NEW ORLEANS CAJUN-STYLE EGGS

Preparation: about 20 minutes   Cook: about 10 minutes

Cajun, or Creole, cooking is a fascinating blend of French, Spanish, African and native Indian cooking. Try this easy egg recipe for a Cajun brunch.

¼ cup	Imperial Margarine	50 mL
3	tomatoes, peeled and chopped	3
1 cup	sliced mushrooms	250 mL
1	medium onion, chopped	1
1	stalk celery, chopped	1
½	green pepper, chopped	½
1	clove garlic, chopped	1
1	can (7½ oz/213 mL) tomato sauce	1
1	OXO Chicken Bouillon Cube	1
½ cup	water	125 mL
½ tsp	EACH: oregano, basil, thyme, Tabasco sauce	2 mL
6	ham slices, halved, heated	6
6	hard-cooked eggs, halved lengthwise	6
6	English muffins, halved and toasted	6

In a medium skillet, over medium-high heat, melt margarine; sauté tomatoes, mushrooms, onion, celery, green pepper and garlic, about 5 minutes. Add tomato sauce, bouillon cube, water and seasonings. Bring to a boil, then reduce heat and simmer until vegetables are tender and sauce is thickened, about 10–15 minutes. On a baking sheet, arrange ham and eggs, cut side down over muffin halves; top with sauce. Bake at 300°F (150°C) about 10 minutes.

Makes 6 servings.

Calories per serving: 390   Iron; vitamins A and C; thiamin: Excellent   Fiber: Good

HOT 'N CREAMY VEGETABLE SANDWICH

Preparation: about 5 minutes   Cook: 20 minutes

When you have run out of quick luncheon ideas, try this delicious topping with split croissants or toasted buns.

1	pouch Lipton 7 Vegetable Soup	1
1	container (500 mL) cottage cheese	1
3	slices bacon, cooked and crumbled	3
8	split croissants or buns	8
¾ cup	grated Black Diamond Cheddar Cheese	175 mL

In a medium casserole, combine soup mix, cottage cheese and bacon. Bake at 350°F (180°C) 20 minutes. Sprinkle Cheddar cheese on top during last 5 minutes.

Makes approximately 8 sandwiches.

TIP: Serve leftovers cold as a sandwich filling with shredded lettuce.

Calories per serving: 276

MEATS

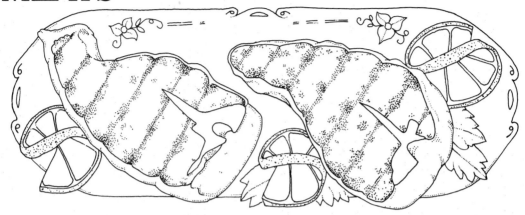

Meat is usually the part of the menu that requires the most planning and cooking, so we have emphasized prepare-ahead and casserole recipes in this section. But there are also recipes for last-minute steaks and chops using marinades. There are even instructions for a roast that cooks in one hour. Two-In-One Beef Stew (page 57) is a particularly convenient recipe that makes it easy to follow the advice of doubling a recipe so you can eat one and freeze one. If you freeze a casserole, line the dish with aluminum foil and freeze the food until it is solid. Remove the casserole, place it in a plastic bag and label. Then you have the dish ready for other uses. Allow the casserole to thaw in the refrigerator or cook it frozen and increase the cooking time by one-half. If you prefer, a meat casserole can be made up and refrigerated up to 24 hours before serving. Add 15 to 20 minutes to the cooking time.

QUICK SEASONING TIPS

In seasoning meat dishes, start with a small quantity of a new herb or spice and taste as you season. For best results, use whole spices in slow-cooking meat dishes and add them at the beginning of the cooking process. Over-seasoning can be corrected by cooking large pieces of potato with the meat mixture. Or place a slice of bread on the surface to absorb some of the extra seasoning.

CREATIVE GARNISHING TIPS

Garnished meat is the focus of any meal. For lunch, try colorful tacos, which are a garnish in themselves. The curved shells are filled with rich brown meat, contrasted with shredded lettuce, tomatoes and cheese. Casseroles can be simply garnished with a cluster of cherry tomatoes and sprigs of celery leaves. Try different garnishes with roasts, such as kumquats with lamb. For a buffet, I often serve a glazed ham. Ask the butcher to slice it and tie it back together into its original shape. When serving, release half of the ham slices and arrange them on the serving platter with the remaining "whole" ham. Use spiced crabapples with watercress around the ham. Or glaze the ham with orange juice and surround the platter with curly endive and orange slices, topped with mounds of cranberry relish. It's a beautifully easy way to serve ham.

CHEESY SKILLET MEATBALLS

Preparation: under 15 minutes   Cook: 15 minutes

Use your shortcut shelf supplies in preparing this easy meatball recipe.

1 lb	lean ground beef	500 g
¼ cup	fine bread crumbs	50 mL
¼ cup	finely chopped onion	50 mL
1	egg, slightly beaten	1
¼ tsp	nutmeg	1 mL
1	pouch Lipton Cheddar Cheese Soup	1
1 cup	water	250 mL
	Hot cooked egg noodles	
	Parsley	

In a medium bowl, combine beef, bread crumbs, onion, egg and nutmeg. Shape into 16 meatballs; place on a baking pan; broil 5 minutes or until brown. In a large saucepan, blend soup mix with water according to package directions. Add meatballs, cover and simmer 15 minutes. Serve over egg noodles and garnish with parsley. Meatballs and sauce may be frozen.

Makes 4 servings.

TIP: When meatballs are cooked in a skillet, it is necessary to turn them as they brown. To cook meatballs quickly without turning, place on a baking pan, bake at 350°F (180°C) for 10–15 minutes or broil until brown.

Calories per serving: 359, without noodles   Iron: Excellent   Protein: Good

MEXICAN TOMATO LASAGNA

Preparation: about 10 minutes   Cook: about 25 minutes

Everyone has tried Italian lasagna. Surprise your family with this Mexican variation by substituting corn tostada shells for lasagna noodles.

1 lb	lean ground beef	500 g
1 tbsp	vegetable oil	15 mL
1	pouch Lipton Onion Soup	1
1 cup	water	250 mL
1	can (7½ oz/213 mL) tomato sauce	1
1	green pepper, chopped	1
2 tsp	EACH: chili powder, oregano, garlic powder	10 mL
2¼ cups	grated Black Diamond Cheddar Cheese, divided	550 mL
1	package MexiCasa Tostada or Taco Shells (10)	1

In a medium skillet, brown ground beef in vegetable oil; drain. Stir in soup mix, water, tomato sauce, green pepper and seasonings. Simmer sauce 5 minutes. In a greased 11 × 7-inch (2 L) baking pan, place 1 cup (250 mL) sauce, 5 tostada shells, overlapped, and half the cheese; repeat layers. Top with ¼ cup (50 mL) cheese. Bake, uncovered, at 350°F (180°C) 20–25 minutes. Let stand 10 minutes. Cut into 6 squares.

Microwave: In a 6-cup (1.5 L) casserole, brown ground beef at HIGH (100%) until crumbly, 5–6 minutes; stir once, drain. Add soup mix, water, tomato sauce, green pepper and seasonings. Heat at HIGH 3–4 minutes. Assemble casserole as above. Heat, covered, at HIGH, 10–15 minutes. Let stand 10 minutes.

Makes 6 servings.

TIP: If lasagna is made early in the day and refrigerated, add 10–15 minutes to the baking time. Or, freeze and defrost before baking.

Calories per serving: 528   Calcium; iron; vitamins A and C: Excellent   Protein: Good

UNSTUFFED CABBAGE ROLLS

Preparation: about 15 minutes   Cook: about 30 minutes

This quick method gives you the same taste as cabbage rolls made in the traditional, time-consuming way.

½ lb	lean ground beef	250 g
1	medium onion, chopped	1
1 tbsp	vegetable oil	15 mL
½ cup	water	125 mL
1	pouch Lipton Chicken Noodle Soup	1
1 cup	sliced mushrooms	250 mL
3 cups	coarsely shredded cabbage	750 mL
½ tsp	EACH: oregano, basil	2 mL
1	can (7½ oz/213 mL) tomato sauce	1
½ cup	water	125 mL

In a small skillet, brown beef and onion in vegetable oil; drain. Stir in water, soup mix and mushrooms. Place mixture in a 6-cup (1.5 L) casserole; top with cabbage. Mix oregano and basil with tomato sauce and water; pour over cabbage. Cover and bake at 350°F (180°C) 30–35 minutes.

Microwave: In a small bowl, brown ground beef and onion in vegetable oil at HIGH (100%) 3–4 minutes; drain. Add water, soup mix and mushrooms. Assemble casserole as above. Heat, covered, at HIGH 12–15 minutes until cabbage is tender. Let stand 5 minutes.

Makes 3–4 servings.

Calories per serving: 305   Iron and vitamin C: Excellent   Vitamin A: Good

CLASSIC LIPTON ONION MEAT LOAF

Preparation: about 5 minutes   Cook: 1 hour

Ground beef and Lipton Onion Soup just naturally go together. This recipe is a favorite in countless households because it makes a meat loaf that's moist and easy to slice. In case you haven't tried it, you'll want to add it and the variation to your collection of special recipes.

1	pouch Lipton Onion Soup	1
1½ lb	ground beef	750 g
2	eggs, beaten	2
¼ cup	ketchup	50 mL
½ cup	fine bread crumbs	125 mL
¾ cup	warm water	175 mL
	Hard-cooked eggs, dill pickles, grated cheese (optional)	

In a medium bowl, combine soup mix with beef. Add remaining ingredients and mix thoroughly.

Place in a 9 × 5-inch (2 L) loaf pan. Place hard-cooked eggs, dill pickles or grated cheese in center of loaf, if desired. Bake at 350°F (180°C) 1 hour. Drain; let stand 10 minutes before slicing. May be frozen.

Microwave: Assemble meat loaf mixture as above. Heat, covered with waxed paper, at HIGH (100%) 12–14 minutes. Let stand 5–10 minutes.

Makes 6 servings.

Calories per serving: 448   Iron: Excellent   Protein: Good

VARIATION

Mexican Meat Loaf: To 1 lb (500 g) ground beef, add 1 package MexiCasa Taco Seasoning Mix combined with 1 tbsp (15 mL) water and 1 beaten egg. Add 1 cup (250 mL) each: soft bread crumbs and cut-up canned tomatoes. Bake as above.

TIP: Place whole canned tomatoes in a measuring cup; cut with kitchen shears, adding tomatoes to make desired amount.

LIPTON ONION BURGERS

One of my favorite Lipton ads suggests this novel approach to an old stand-by: "More people barbecue our soups than any other. Once you taste this delicious Lipton Onion Burger you'll understand why." And while you're at it, try the various toppings.

HAMBURGERS

Combine 1 pouch Lipton Onion Soup and 1½ lb (750 g) ground meat. Mix completely.

Form mixture into 6 patties. Cook as desired.

SUGGESTED SOUP AND MEAT COMBINATIONS

For ground beef: Onion, or Onion-Mushroom Soup. For ground pork: Onion-Mushroom, or Golden Onion Soup.

TIP: Shape hamburger patties with wet hands for an extra-fast and neat job.

BURGER TOPPINGS

Mexican Fiesta Burgers: Top each cooked burger with MexiCasa Taco Relish, shredded lettuce and grated Cheddar cheese.

Typically British Burgers: Top each cooked burger with a strip of cooked bacon and a cheese slice. Serve on an English muffin.

Burgers à la Française: Combine softened cream cheese with Roquefort or blue cheese and milk. Use as a topping for cooked burgers with a tomato slice and Dijon mustard.

California Burgers: Top cooked burgers with sliced avocado, sweet onion rings and alfalfa sprouts.

Hawaiian Burgers: Top each cooked burger with a pineapple slice, chopped green onions and mayonnaise. Sprinkle with sesame seeds.

Italian Burgers: Sprinkle cooked burgers with basil and oregano, top with sliced mushrooms, Mozzarella cheese and a tomato slice.

Cajun (Creole) Burgers: Sprinkle burgers during cooking with a Cajun seasoning blend consisting of: ½ tsp (2 mL) each: garlic salt, white and black pepper, cayenne pepper and ¼ tsp (1 mL) dry mustard.

Makes 6 servings.

TIP: Try stuffing the patties with any of the following: cream cheese and pickle; Cheddar cheese; hard-cooked eggs; Mozzarella cheese and ketchup. Make a hollow in the patty, fill with stuffing, fold meat over the filling and seal well.

Calories per serving: 377, without topping   Iron: Excellent   Protein: Good

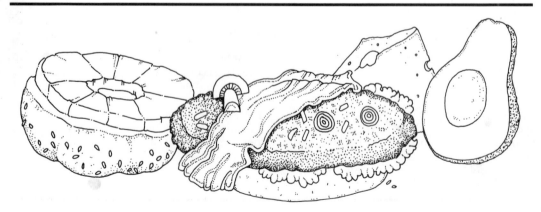

CORDON BLEU ECONOMY BEEF ROLLS

Preparation: about 15 minutes   Cook: about 40 minutes

To give a Cordon Bleu treatment to ground beef, try this quick and easy entrée. It's an elegant but economical dish for family or guests.

2	eggs, slightly beaten	2
2	pouches Lipton Onion *or* Onion-Mushroom Soup	2
½ cup	oatmeal	125 mL
2 lb	lean ground beef	1 kg
4	thin slices Black Diamond Mozzarella Cheese	4
4	slices bacon, halved	4
1 cup	water	250 mL
¼ cup	red wine	50 mL
2 tbsp	all-purpose flour	25 mL

In a medium bowl, combine eggs, 1 pouch soup mix, oatmeal and ground beef. Pat into eight 4-inch (10 cm) square patties. Place 1 cheese slice and ½ bacon slice on each patty. Roll up, jelly roll style, making sure cheese and bacon are completely enclosed. On a lightly greased baking sheet, bake rolls at 350°F (180°C) 35–40 minutes. Meanwhile, prepare sauce. In a small saucepan, combine 1 pouch soup mix, water, wine and flour. Cook, stirring constantly, until smooth and thickened. Serve with beef rolls. May be frozen.

Microwave: Assemble meat patties as above. Heat bacon at HIGH (100%) 2–3 minutes until partially cooked. Place 1 cheese slice and ½ bacon slice on each patty. Roll up, making sure cheese and bacon are completely enclosed. Arrange in an 8-inch (2 L) square baking dish. Heat, covered, at MEDIUM (50%) 20–25 minutes, or until beef is cooked; turn and rearrange rolls after 10 minutes. Let stand, covered, 5–10 minutes. Prepare sauce as above.

Makes 8 servings.

TIP: To separate thin slices of bacon, simply roll up the package crosswise before you open it. The slices will separate easily.

Calories per serving: 374   Iron: Excellent   Protein: Good

BEEF AND VEGETABLE PACKAGES

Preparation: about 10 minutes   Cook: about 25 minutes

Avid campers or barbecuers like this popular recipe. Individual servings of meat and vegetables are cooked in foil packets on the barbecue grill over the coals or in the oven.

1 lb	blade *or* cross-rib steak, about 1 inch (2.5 cm) thick	500 g
1	pouch Lipton Onion Soup	1
1 tbsp	EACH: water, Worcestershire sauce, vinegar, honey	15 mL
1 tsp	prepared *or* Dijon mustard	5 mL
2	potatoes, quartered	2
2	carrots, quartered	2

On a barbecue grill, sear meat on both sides over hot coals; set aside. In a small bowl, mix together 3 tbsp (45 mL) soup mix, water, Worcestershire sauce, vinegar, honey and mustard. Brush on both sides of the steak. Place steak in center of a length of foil. Arrange vegetables on top of steak. Wrap securely with double folds on top and turn sides up to prevent leakage. Bake packaged steak and vegetables over medium coals about 20–25 minutes or in 350°F (180°C) oven until meat and vegetables are tender. (Check by unfolding a small section of foil on top and pierce meat with a long fork; be careful not to let sauce run out.) Turn package periodically during cooking. When tender, carefully remove vegetables, meat and sauce to serving plates.

Makes 4 servings.

TIP : Remaining soup mix may be added to 1 cup (250 mL) dairy sour cream to make a refreshing dip.

Calories per serving: 642   Vitamins A and C; iron; niacin: Excellent   Protein: Good

SUMMER SIZZLE BARBECUE SAUCE

Preparation: about 5 minutes   Cook: 20 minutes

When you're barbecuing, it saves valuable time to use a sauce recipe that can double as a marinade by simply adding red wine.

1	pouch Lipton Onion Soup	1
½ cup	EACH: ketchup, water	125 mL
¼ cup	vinegar	50 mL
2 tbsp	honey	25 mL
1 tsp	dry mustard	5 mL
¼ tsp	chili powder	1 mL
1–2 tsp	Worcestershire sauce	5–10 mL

In a medium saucepan, combine all ingredients. Bring to a boil, then reduce heat and simmer, uncovered, 20 minutes. Cool, cover and store in refrigerator.

Calories per 1 tbsp (15 mL): 25

Microwave: In a 6-cup (1.5 L) covered casserole, combine all ingredients. Heat at HIGH (100%) 3–5 minutes; stir twice. Let stand, covered, 5 minutes before serving.

Makes approximately 1 cup (250 mL).

TIP: This sauce is wonderful as a barbecue baste, brushed on chicken, pork chops, ribs or steaks, hamburgers, beef or pork kabobs. It can also be used during oven baking or broiling. Brush on at beginning of cooking or part way through.

VARIATION

Summer Sizzle Marinade: Dilute prepared sauce with ½ cup (125 mL) red wine. Marinate meat 2–3 hours at room temperature or overnight in refrigerator.

Makes approximately 1½ cups (375 mL).

ONE-HOUR BEEF ROAST

Preparation: under 5 minutes   Cook: 1 hour

A roast that can be done in an hour is a boon to a busy cook. When the Beef Information Centre's home economist wanted to develop a method to cook beef "in a hurry," she consulted with the Lipton Consumer Test Kitchen staff. This recipe gives you a tender, succulent roast.

3 lb	sirloin tip, rump *or* round roast	1.5 kg
1	pouch Lipton Onion Soup	1
½ tsp	thyme	2 mL
¼ tsp	garlic powder	1 mL
2 cups	hot water, red wine *or* apple juice	500 mL

Place roast in a roasting pan. Rub 3 tbsp (45 mL) soup mix into roast. Season with thyme and garlic. Add liquid, cover and cook at 500°F (260°C) 20 minutes. Reduce heat to 325°F (160°C) and cook for remaining 40 minutes.

Calories per serving: 677   Iron: Excellent   Protein: Good

If roast is more than 3 lb (1.5 kg), allow additional 10 minutes per ½ lb (250 g) at 325°F (160°C). If desired, prepare gravy. Add remaining soup mix for additional flavor.

Makes 6–8 servings.

TIPS: When a roast is put into the oven, set a small foil pan partly filled with flour beside it. When the flour has browned, it's ready for flavorful brown gravy making. If you're a make-ahead cook, you can take the same roast, sprinkle it with a package of onion soup mix and roast it in foil at 200°F (100°C) for 9 hours.

TWO-IN-ONE BEEF STEW

Preparation: about 10 minutes   Cook: about 40 minutes

Make a large batch of this beef stew and freeze it for two hurry-up dinners. On a busy day, serve either Busy Day Stew or Bavarian Stew with hot crusty bread. The choice is yours.

3 lb	boneless stewing beef, cubed	1.5 kg
¼ cup	EACH: all-purpose flour, vegetable oil	50 mL
2	pouches Lipton Onion Soup	2
2 cups	water *or* tomato juice	500 mL

In a plastic bag, toss meat in flour. In a large skillet, over medium-high heat, brown beef in hot oil. Combine soup mix and water; add to skillet. Bring to a boil, then reduce heat, cover and simmer 40 minutes. Extra liquid may be added if required. Remove from heat and cool. Divide and package for the freezer.

BUSY DAY STEW   Preparation: about 15 minutes   Cook: about 35 minutes

1	package Beef Stew, thawed	1
½ tsp	caraway seeds (optional)	2 mL
1	can (19 oz/540 mL) tomatoes, undrained	1
4	carrots, peeled, cut in bite-size pieces	4
3	medium potatoes, peeled and cubed	3
1 cup	EACH: whole kernel corn, frozen peas *or* frozen cut green beans	250 mL

In a large saucepan, combine stew, caraway seeds, tomatoes, carrots and potatoes. Bring to a boil, then reduce heat, cover and simmer about 25 minutes or until vegetables and meat are tender. Add extra liquid if required. Add corn and peas. Simmer, covered, another 10 minutes.

Makes 6 servings.

Calories per serving: 521   Iron; vitamins A and C: Excellent   Thiamin and protein: Good

---

BAVARIAN STEW   Preparation: about 10 minutes   Cook: about 10 minutes

1	package Beef Stew, thawed	1
1 cup	tomato juice, beef bouillon *or* water	250 mL
2 tbsp	ketchup	25 mL
2 cups	coarsely chopped cabbage	500 mL
1	can (10 oz/284 mL) whole mushrooms, undrained	1
1 cup	dairy sour cream	250 mL
	Hot cooked egg noodles	

In a large saucepan, combine stew, liquid, ketchup, cabbage and mushrooms. Bring to a boil, then reduce heat, cover and simmer about 10 minutes or until cabbage is tender-crisp. Stir in sour cream and serve over noodles.

Makes 6 servings.

Calories per serving: 469, without noodles   Iron and vitamin C: Excellent   Vitamin A and protein: Good

BEEF STROGANOFF

Preparation: about 15 minutes   Cook: 1 hour

When a Russian count from one of St. Petersburg's prominent families wanted a light, after-theater supper dish, Beef Stroganoff was created. This low-calorie recipe is one of the many variations.

1 tbsp	all-purpose flour	15 mL
1/4 tsp	EACH: salt, pepper, nutmeg	1 mL
1 lb	lean beef (flank or round steak), cut into 1 × 2-inch (2.5 cm × 5 cm) strips	500 g
3 tbsp	Becel Margarine	45 mL
1	medium onion, chopped	1
1-2 cups	sliced mushrooms	250–500 mL
1	OXO Beef Bouillon Cube	1
1 cup	boiling water	250 mL
1/4 cup	tomato paste	50 mL
1/2 cup	low-fat plain yogurt	125 mL
	Hot cooked egg noodles *or* rice	

In a plastic bag, combine flour, salt, pepper and nutmeg. Toss beef strips in flour mixture. In a medium skillet, over medium-high heat, brown beef in melted margarine. Add onion and mushrooms and cook briefly. Dissolve bouillon cube in boiling water. Add stock and tomato paste to skillet. Bring to a boil; remove to a casserole dish. Bake, covered, at 350°F (180°C) 1 hour or until tender. Stir occasionally. May be frozen at this stage. Stir in yogurt and serve over noodles.

Microwave: Prepare beef as above. In an 8-cup (2 L) covered casserole, melt margarine at HIGH (100%) 45–60 seconds. Add beef; heat, covered, at HIGH 5 minutes; stir once. Add onion and mushrooms; heat at HIGH 4–5 minutes. Dissolve bouillon cube in boiling water. Add stock and tomato paste to meat. Heat, covered, at HIGH 10–15 minutes; stir occasionally. Let stand 5–10 minutes. Stir in yogurt and serve over noodles.

Makes 4 servings.

Calories per serving: 372, without noodles or rice   Iron: Excellent   Vitamins A and C; protein: Good

FILLET OF BEEF WITH PARSLEY STUFFING

Preparation: about 10 minutes   Cook: 45 minutes

Try this beef tenderloin with parsley stuffing for an unusual entrée for company or a special family dinner.

6	green onions, finely chopped	6
6	mushrooms, finely chopped	6
1 tbsp	Becel Margarine	15 mL
1/2 cup	soft bread crumbs	125 mL
1/2 cup	fresh parsley, finely chopped	125 mL
	Freshly ground black pepper	
2 lb	beef tenderloin, trimmed of all fat	1 kg

In a skillet, over medium-high heat, sauté green onions and mushrooms in melted margarine until soft, 1–2 minutes. Add bread crumbs and cook until golden brown. Add parsley and pepper; remove from heat and cool. Make a pocket lengthways through the beef fillet and fill cavity with the stuffing. Secure with skewers or string. Place beef on a rack in a baking dish; add a little water. Bake at 350°F (180°C) 45 minutes or until desired doneness is reached.

Makes 8 servings.

Calories per serving: 358   Iron and vitamin A: Excellent   Protein: Good

PORK CHOPS AND PEACHES

Preparation: about 10 minutes   Cook: about 45 minutes

Top thick pork chops with warmed peaches for a mouth-watering entrée.

4	pork chops, 1 inch (2.5 cm) thick	4
2 tbsp	vegetable oil	25 mL
½ tsp	ginger	2 mL
2 tbsp	honey	25 mL
1	pouch Lipton Onion-Mushroom Soup	1
1 cup	water	250 mL
¼ cup	cider vinegar	50 mL
2 tbsp	cornstarch (optional)	25 mL
2 tbsp	water (optional)	25 mL
½ cup	sliced peaches, drained	125 mL

In a medium skillet, over medium-high heat, brown pork chops in hot oil on each side; drain. Combine ginger, honey, soup mix, water and vinegar. Pour over pork chops. Cover skillet and simmer 30–40 minutes or until tender. Thicken sauce with cornstarch and water if desired. Top meat with peach slices; heat 5 minutes to warm fruit.

Microwave: Heat pork chops in oil in an 8-inch (2 L) square baking dish at HIGH (100%) 3–4 minutes. Turn once. Combine ginger, honey, soup mix, water and vinegar; pour over pork chops. Heat, covered, at MEDIUM (50%) 15–20 minutes; turn part way through. Thicken sauce if desired. Top meat with peach slices; heat, covered, at HIGH (100%) 1–2 minutes. Let stand, covered, 5 minutes.

Makes 4 servings.

Calories per serving: 467   Thiamin: Excellent   Protein: Good

STIR-FRY PORK TENDERLOIN AND VEGETABLES

Preparation: about 10 minutes   Cook: about 10 minutes

Stir-frying is a fast cooking method for the busy cook. Cut up meat and vegetables, stir-fry in a wok or skillet, and serve an attractive meal in a matter of minutes.

1	pouch Lipton Bon Appétit French Onion Soup	1
1 cup	water	250 mL
2 tbsp	dry sherry	25 mL
1 tbsp	EACH: soy sauce, cornstarch	15 mL
1 lb	pork tenderloin, cut in thin strips	500 g
3 tbsp	vegetable oil	45 mL
1	medium zucchini, cut in sticks	1
1½ cups	diagonally sliced celery	375 mL
1 cup	sliced mushrooms	250 mL
½ cup	EACH: red and yellow pepper strips	125 mL
	Hot cooked rice	

In a small bowl, combine soup mix, water, sherry, soy sauce and cornstarch. In a wok or large skillet, over medium-high heat, brown meat in hot oil; set aside. Add each vegetable and stir-fry over high heat until tender-crisp; set aside. Return meat and vegetables and add sauce; cook and stir until thickened, approximately 3–4 minutes. Serve with rice.

Makes 3–4 servings.

Calories per serving: 611, without rice   Thiamin: Excellent   Iron, protein and vitamin C: Good

ORIENTAL MARINATED PORK

Preparation: about 5 minutes   Marinate: 3 hours or overnight
Cook: 2½ hours or about 7 hours in a slow cooker

For quick planning at its best, start this roast in your slow cooker when you leave in the morning and enjoy the lovely aroma of a ready-to-serve meal when you arrive home.

3–4 lb	**boneless pork shoulder** *or* **butt roast**	1.5–2 kg
¼ cup	**EACH: soy sauce, dry sherry**	50 mL
2	**cloves garlic, minced**	2
1	**pouch Lipton Onion Soup**	1
1 tsp	**EACH: dry mustard, ground ginger**	5 mL
½ tsp	**thyme**	2 mL

Place pork roast in a large bowl. In a small bowl, combine remaining ingredients. Pour over roast. Marinate 3 hours at room temperature or overnight in the refrigerator. Transfer roast and marinade into a roasting pan or a slow cooker. Cover and roast at 325°F (160°C) 2–2½ hours or 6–7 hours at medium setting in a slow cooker. Gravy may be thickened with flour if desired.

Makes 4–5 servings.

Calories per serving: 843   Iron, protein and thiamin: Excellent

ONION BREAD COATING

Meal preparation speeds up when you have a ready-to-use coating mix for chicken pieces, pork chops, fish or veal. Give an international flair to your menus by varying this basic recipe.

1	**pouch Lipton Onion Soup**	1
1 cup	**coarse bread crumbs**	250 mL

Combine soup mix and bread crumbs. Store in a tightly covered container. Use to coat chicken pieces, pork chops, fish or veal chops. Brush meat with oil and dip both sides in coating; pat a little extra on upper surface. Bake or pan fry as desired.

Makes 1¼ cups (300 mL).

VARIATIONS

Oriental Coating: Use Golden Onion *or* Onion-Mushroom Soup, add ginger to bread coating, sprinkle meat with soy sauce. Pat coating onto meat.
Polynesian Coating: Use Onion-Mushroom Soup and add lemon *or* orange rind.

Indian Coating: Add curry powder to basic recipe.

TIP: Use Onion, Onion-Mushroom or Golden Onion Soup to flavor bread stuffing for whole turkey or chicken.

TOURTIÈRE

Preparation: 45 minutes   Cook: 50 minutes

In Quebec, as well as many parts of English Canada, tourtière is traditionally served on Christmas Eve. A friend has her own version of this tradition. She freezes several tourtières before the holiday season and serves them with turkey and ham, salads, rolls and Christmas sweets on Boxing Day. She says it's an easy way to entertain twenty or more.

1 lb	lean ground pork	500 g
½ lb	ground veal	250 g
1	pouch Lipton Onion Soup	1
1	clove garlic, chopped	1
¼ tsp	EACH: pepper, sage, cloves	1 mL
½ cup	boiling water	125 mL
3	medium potatoes, boiled and mashed	3
	Pastry for double crust 9-inch (23 cm) pie	

In a medium covered saucepan, over medium heat, cook pork, veal, soup mix, garlic, seasonings and water for 45 minutes; stir occasionally. Add mashed potatoes to cooked meat; cool. Line pie plate with pastry; add cooled meat mixture. Top with second crust, seal edges, flute and make cutouts in surface or slash pastry to allow steam to escape. Bake at 450°F (220°C) 10 minutes, reduce heat to 350°F (180°C) and bake 30–40 minutes.

Makes 6 servings.

Calories per serving: 645   Thiamin: Excellent   Iron, protein and riboflavin: Good

SHERRIED CREAMED HAM

Preparation: about 10 minutes   Cook: 10 minutes

For a luncheon or brunch, try this sherried ham over patty shells. It freezes well, so you can make it ahead and reheat it for relaxed entertaining.

2 tbsp	chopped green pepper	25 mL
¼ cup	chopped onion	50 mL
½ cup	sliced mushrooms	125 mL
2 tbsp	margarine or butter, melted	25 mL
1	pouch Lipton Bon Appétit Cream of Chicken Soup	1
1½ cups	water	375 mL
½ cup	milk	125 mL
1½ cups	cubed, cooked ham, chicken, turkey or pork	375 mL
2 tbsp	drained and chopped pimiento	25 mL
1 tbsp	dry sherry (optional)	15 mL
	Patty shells or hot cooked rice	

In a medium skillet, over medium-high heat, sauté green pepper, onion and mushrooms in margarine for 5 minutes. In a medium saucepan, combine soup mix and water. Bring to a boil, then reduce heat and simmer 5 minutes, stirring frequently. Add milk, ham, pimiento, sherry and vegetable mixture. Reheat to serving temperature. Serve over patty shells or rice.

Microwave: In a 6-cup (1.5 L) casserole, melt margarine at HIGH (100%) 45 seconds. Add green pepper, onion and mushrooms; heat at HIGH 3–4 minutes. In a 4-cup (1 L) glass measure, heat soup mix and 1 cup (250 mL) water at HIGH 3 minutes; stir frequently. Add soup, milk, ham, pimiento and sherry to vegetables. Heat and serve.

Makes 3–4 servings.

Calories per serving: 209, without patty shells or rice   Vitamin C and thiamin: Excellent

THREE-IN-ONE VEAL AND ZUCCHINI

Preparation: about 10 minutes   Cook: about 25 minutes

This three-in-one recipe can be served as an appetizer, a buffet dish or an elegant entrée. The manner in which you garnish and present it makes the difference.

2 tbsp	all-purpose flour	25 mL
1/2 tsp	marjoram *or* basil	2 mL
1/4 tsp	thyme	1 mL
1 lb	stewing veal, diced	500 g
2 tbsp	vegetable oil	25 mL
2 cups	water	500 mL
1	pouch Lipton Bon Appétit Minestrone Soup	1
1	zucchini, cut into strips	1
	Black Diamond Grated Parmesan Cheese	
	Hot cooked noodles (optional)	

In a plastic bag, combine flour and seasonings. Toss veal cubes in flour mixture. In a large skillet, over medium-high heat, brown veal in oil. Add water; simmer, covered, 10–15 minutes or until veal is almost tender. Stir in soup mix and continue simmering an additional 10 minutes. May be frozen at this stage. Add zucchini during last 5 minutes. Sprinkle liberally with Parmesan cheese just before serving. Serve over noodles, if desired.

Microwave: Prepare veal as above. In an 8-cup (2 L) covered casserole, heat oil at HIGH (100%) 2 minutes. Add veal, heat at HIGH 4–5 minutes; stir once. Add water, heat at HIGH 4–5 minutes. Stir in soup mix; heat at MEDIUM (50%) 10–15 minutes until veal is almost tender; stir occasionally. Add zucchini; heat at MEDIUM 3 minutes. Let stand 5–10 minutes.

Makes 3–4 servings.

TIPS: 1. For an appetizer, cut the veal into small cubes and serve in cooked zucchini shells. 2. Serve Three-In-One Veal on noodles in a chafing dish with grated Parmesan on the side for self-serving buffets. 3. Excellent as a light, special occasion entrée served on a bed of shredded, lightly steamed spinach or simply presented on fine china and garnished with fresh herbs.

Calories per serving: 442, without noodles   Iron: Excellent   Vitamin C and protein: Good

APRICOT-STUFFED LAMB CHOPS

Preparation: 10 minutes   Marinate: 2 hours   Cook: 35 minutes

These chops stuffed with apricots are further enhanced by the use of a marinade.

4	loin lamb chops, 2-inch (5 cm) thick	4
4	dried apricots, halved	4
1	pouch Lipton Onion *or* Onion-Mushroom Soup	1
1 cup	water	250 mL
1/4 cup	olive *or* vegetable oil	50 mL
1/4 cup	honey	50 mL
2 tbsp	Dijon mustard	25 mL
2 tsp	rosemary	10 mL
1/2 tsp	ground ginger	2 mL

With knife parallel to cutting board, make a 1-inch (2.5 cm) wide by 1-inch (2.5 cm) deep cut in meaty side of each chop. Into each cut insert 2 apricot halves; press firmly to close. In shallow baking dish, combine remaining ingredients; add chops and turn to coat. Cover and marinate in refrigerator, turning occasionally, at least 2 hours. Bake chops at 425°F (220°C) 35 minutes. Baste with marinade and turn chops occasionally.

Makes 4 servings.

Calories per serving: 397   Iron and protein: Good

VEAL WITH FRESH MUSHROOM SAUCE

Preparation: about 15 minutes   Cook: about 20 minutes

In most veal recipes, chicken can be substituted to make a more economical meat dish. You won't even miss salt, when you have the savoury flavors of onions, wine and mushrooms.

1 lb	veal for scaloppine	500 g
¼ cup	all-purpose flour	50 mL
¼ tsp	freshly ground black pepper	1 mL
⅛ tsp	salt (optional)	0.5 mL
¼ cup	Becel Margarine, divided	50 mL
1	large onion, chopped	1
2 cups	sliced mushrooms	500 mL
2 cups	chicken broth	500 mL
½ cup	dry white wine	125 mL
3 cups	cooked white rice	750 mL

Pound veal slices very thin. On a flat plate, combine flour, pepper and salt. Coat veal with flour mixture; shake off excess; reserve flour. In a large skillet, over medium-high heat, sauté veal in 2 tbsp (25 mL) melted margarine until well browned on both sides. Remove and keep warm. Add remaining margarine; sauté onion 5 minutes. Add mushrooms; cook, stirring fre-quently, until mushrooms are tender and juices have evaporated, about 5 minutes. Combine reserved flour with chicken broth and wine. Stir into skillet, bring to a boil, cook and stir until smooth and thickened (extra flour may be used for thicker gravy). Return veal to skillet and cook for 15–20 minutes or until tender. May be frozen at this stage. Serve over rice.

Microwave: Prepare veal as above. In a 12 × 8-inch (3 L) covered casserole, melt margarine at HIGH (100%) 45–60 seconds. Add veal, onion and mushrooms; heat, covered, at HIGH 12–15 minutes. Combine reserved flour with chicken broth and wine. Stir into casserole; heat at HIGH 4–5 minutes, stirring several times. Let stand, covered, 5 minutes.

Makes 4 servings.

Calories per serving: 567   Iron and thiamin: Excellent   Fiber, protein and riboflavin: Good

DILL LAMB SHISH KABOBS

Preparation: about 15 minutes   Cook: 30 minutes

Experiment with herbs in your cooking to give a quick and subtle change to your recipes. Rosemary is generally used with lamb, but try dill and enjoy the difference.

¼ cup	Becel Margarine, melted	50 mL
2 tsp	dried dill weed	10 mL
	or	
2 tbsp	fresh dill weed	25 mL
1	clove garlic, minced	1
	Juice of 1 lemon	
1 lb	boneless lamb, cubed	500 g
8	medium fresh mushrooms	8
1	medium zucchini, sliced	1
1	medium green, yellow or red pepper, cubed	1
2	carrots, sliced, partially cooked	2

In a small bowl, combine margarine, dill, garlic and lemon juice. On 4 skewers, alternately thread lamb with vegetables. Brush with herb mixture. Place skewers on barbecue grill over medium coals; cook 30 minutes or until desired doneness is reached; baste and turn as required.

Makes 4 kabobs.

TIP: Vegetables cook faster than meat. If you cook meat to the rare stage, the vegetables will not overcook. If you want well-done meat, place vegetables on separate skewers and cook for a shorter length of time.

Calories per serving: 557   Vitamins A and C: Excellent   Iron, protein, fiber and thiamin: Good

POULTRY

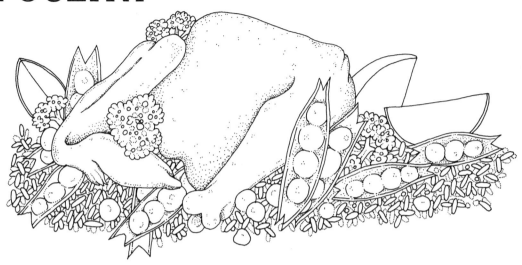

Chicken used to be reserved for Sunday dinners, but it is now enjoyed seven days of the week. It combines well with many flavors including wine, herbs, yogurt, sour cream, juices, bouillons, fruits and most vegetables. Ten-Minute Tarragon Chicken (page 67) is a quick family supper and Jeweled Chicken (page 72) is easy company fare. Turkey was once reserved for Christmas and New Year's. As a young girl, my grandfather always ordered another turkey for my birthday dinner in early January. Today, happily, turkey is readily available and economical as well. A true shortcut to cooking is the preparation of casseroles from leftover turkey — and this should not be practised only at holiday times.

QUICK SEASONING TIPS

Because of the delicate flavor of poultry, it is important to season it with care — particularly when cooking in the microwave oven. Always use slightly less seasoning than the recipe calls for and correct the seasoning after the food has finished cooking. Also, reduce salt in any recipe calling for more than 1 tsp (5 mL). Since small cuts of poultry cook quickly when they are microwaved, sprinkle with Lawry's Seasoned Salt, which contains paprika. It acts as an aid in browning and improves the pale appearance of poultry.

CREATIVE GARNISHING TIPS

Garnishes don't have to be exotic to be attractive. Use canned goods such as apricots and cranberry jelly or dried fruits from your shortcut shelf. Place glazed Apricot Onion Chicken (page 69) on a serving platter and surround it with apricot halves filled with cranberry or crabapple jelly. For contrast, use green onion fans. Cut onions into short lengths, snip both ends in thin strips about 1-inch (2.5 cm) long and place them in ice water to curl. Chicken is also attractive garnished with mint leaves and clusters of green grapes and prunes.

CHILI CHICKEN

Preparation: about 10 minutes   Cook: about 40 minutes

Chicken combines well with many different seasonings. This Chili Chicken is equally good served cold. Remember it for a picnic because it can be prepared ahead of time and is so easy to pack.

1/3 cup	EACH: yellow cornmeal, all-purpose flour	75 mL
1 tbsp	chili powder	15 mL
1/2 tsp	ground cumin	2 mL
1/2 tsp	Lawry's Garlic Salt with Parsley	2 mL
2	egg whites, lightly beaten	2
4	boneless chicken breasts, skinned, cut into small fingers	4
1/4 cup	Becel Margarine, melted	50 mL

In a plastic bag, combine cornmeal, flour, chili powder, cumin and garlic salt. In a small bowl, beat egg whites until frothy. Coat chicken pieces completely with egg whites and then with cornmeal mixture. Place chicken in a single layer on a lightly greased, shallow baking pan. Press any remaining cornmeal mixture onto chicken with the back of a spoon. Drizzle chicken evenly with margarine. Bake at 350°F (180°C) 40–50 minutes or until chicken is cooked thoroughly.

Microwave: Prepare chicken as above. Heat at HIGH (100%) 12–15 minutes. Let stand 5 minutes.

Makes 4 servings.

TIP: If I'm going on a picnic, I often freeze a plastic container of water or juice. By the time I arrive, it's thawed and it has kept any perishable picnic items, such as chicken, safe and cool. As well, the thawed liquid provides a refreshing drink.

Calories per serving: 319   Vitamin A and protein: Good

NICE 'N EASY CHICKEN BAKE

Preparation: about 5 minutes   Cook: about 40 minutes

An elegant version of an old favorite is dressed up for company with wine and sour cream.

2 lb	chicken pieces *or*	1 kg
2 1/2–3 lb	broiler-fryer chicken, cut up	1.25–1.5 kg
1	pouch Lipton Onion-Mushroom Soup	1
1/2 cup	dry white wine, sherry *or* apple juice	125 mL
1 tbsp	all-purpose flour	15 mL
1/2 cup	dairy sour cream	125 mL
	Hot cooked noodles *or* rice	

In a shallow baking pan, arrange chicken pieces. Combine soup mix and liquid; pour over chicken; cover with foil. Bake at 350°F (180°C) 35–40 minutes or until chicken is tender. Remove chicken to a serving platter; skim fat from remaining liquid. Combine flour and sour cream; add to liquid. Simmer, stirring constantly until smooth and thickened. Pour sauce over chicken. Serve over noodles or rice.

Microwave: Prepare chicken and sauce in a shallow baking pan as above. Cover with waxed paper and heat at HIGH (100%) 10 minutes. Rearrange and heat at HIGH 8–10 minutes more. Remove and keep warm. Combine flour and sour cream; add to liquid; heat at HIGH 1–2 minutes until thickened. Pour over chicken.

Makes 4–5 servings.

Calories per serving: 529, without noodles or rice   Protein: Excellent

CHICKEN CACCIATORE

Preparation: about 15 minutes   Cook: about 1 hour

Cacciatore means "hunter's style." When chicken is simmered by this Italian method of cooking, it is browned first in margarine or oil and then slowly cooked with seasonings and tomatoes. A salad and noodles complete this dinner.

1½ lb	chicken breasts, split, skinned, boned	750 g
½ cup	all-purpose flour	125 mL
1 tsp	salt	5 mL
¼ tsp	pepper	1 mL
⅓ cup	Becel Margarine	75 mL
1	clove garlic, minced	1
1	medium onion, thinly sliced	1
1	medium green pepper, coarsely chopped	1
1	can (10 oz/284 mL) sliced mushrooms, drained	1
	or	
1½ cups	sliced fresh mushrooms	375 mL
1	can (19 oz/540 mL) tomatoes, undrained	1
½ tsp	salt	2 mL
⅛ tsp	pepper	0.5 mL
½ tsp	EACH: oregano, thyme	2 mL

In a plastic bag, shake chicken in combined flour, salt and pepper, to coat each piece evenly. In a large skillet, over medium-high heat, brown chicken on both sides in melted margarine. Remove chicken; set aside. Add garlic, onion, green pepper and mushrooms; cook gently until tender. Add tomatoes, salt, pepper, oregano and thyme to vegetable mixture. Return chicken to skillet, cover and simmer until chicken is very tender, about 1 hour. If mixture is too thick, thin by adding water or mushroom liquid.

Microwave: Brown chicken as above. Place in an 8-cup (2 L) covered casserole. Stir remaining ingredients together; pour over chicken. Heat, covered, at HIGH (100%) 16–18 minutes; turn and stir twice. Let stand, covered, 5–10 minutes.

Makes 4–6 servings.

Calories per serving: 348   Vitamin C: Excellent   Iron, protein and vitamin A: Good

TEN-MINUTE TARRAGON CHICKEN

Preparation: about 10 minutes   Cook: about 10 minutes

This ten-minute dish is a fast family or company meal, particularly when it is prepared ahead and reheated.

1	medium apple, chopped	1
2 tbsp	margarine, melted	25 mL
2 tbsp	all-purpose flour	25 mL
1 tbsp	tarragon	15 mL
1	pouch Lipton Golden Onion *or* Onion-Mushroom Soup	1
1½ cups	milk	375 mL
4 cups	cubed, cooked chicken *or* turkey	1 L
1 cup	frozen peas	250 mL
3/4 cup	dairy sour cream	175 mL
	Hot cooked noodles *or* rice	

In a skillet, sauté apple in margarine. Add flour, tarragon, and soup mix; blend well. Gradually add milk; cook and stir until smooth and thickened. Stir in chicken and peas; continue to cook until mixture is heated through. Add sour cream; cook and stir just until reheated. Serve over noodles or rice.

Makes 5–6 servings.

TIP: Make ahead and refrigerate, just until ready to serve. Return to skillet or microwave and cook until reheated.

Calories per serving: 334, without noodles or rice   Calcium, protein, iron and vitamin A: Good

DIVINE CHICKEN STROGANOFF

Preparation: about 10 minutes   Cook: about 25 minutes

This prepare-ahead recipe is a favorite of mine for mid-week entertaining. Poach the chicken ahead of time. At the last minute, cook the Noodles & Sauce, and serve.

2	whole chicken breasts, split, skinned, boned and pounded	2
	Salt and pepper	
1	package (300 g) frozen broccoli spears, partially thawed	1
1 cup	water	250 mL
½ cup	dry white wine	125 mL
2 tbsp	margarine *or* butter	25 mL
1	package Lipton Noodles & Sauce—Stroganoff	1
½ cup	milk	125 mL
3 tbsp	chopped pimiento	45 mL

Lightly season chicken with salt and pepper. Top chicken with broccoli; roll up and fasten with toothpicks. In a medium skillet, bring water, wine and margarine to a boil; add chicken, reduce heat, cover and simmer 15–20 minutes or until tender. Remove chicken and keep warm. Stir in noodles and sauce mix, milk and pimiento; boil over medium heat for 5 minutes, stirring occasionally. Return chicken to skillet. Cook an additional 2–3 minutes or until sauce is thickened and noodles are tender.

Microwave: Assemble chicken and broccoli as above. In a 6-cup (1.5 L) covered casserole, bring water, wine and margarine to a boil at HIGH (100%). Add chicken; heat, covered, at HIGH 8–10 minutes or until tender. Remove chicken, keep warm. Stir in remaining ingredients. Heat, uncovered, at HIGH 4–5 minutes, stirring once. Let stand, covered, 5 minutes. Stir and serve with chicken.

Makes 4 servings.

TIP: Pounding a boned chicken breast flattens it so that it will cook evenly and quickly. Place a boned chicken breast between pieces of plastic wrap. Pound with the flat side of a heavy cleaver or a meat pounder, moving from the center out to the edges so it is of even thickness.

Calories per serving: 393   Vitamins A and C: Excellent   Fiber, protein and iron: Good

SWEET 'N SOUR BAKED CHICKEN

Preparation: about 10 minutes   Cook: 1 hour

Sweet 'n sour recipes are often used in Asian and African cooking. Prepare this sauce ahead and freeze or store in the refrigerator until ready to use.

2–3 lb	chicken, cut into serving pieces	1–1.5 kg
1	pouch Lipton Onion Soup	1
¼ cup	brown sugar	50 mL
½ cup	tomato sauce	125 mL
¼ cup	EACH: water, vinegar	50 mL
1 cup	crushed pineapple, undrained	250 mL

In a 12 × 8-inch (3 L) baking pan, arrange chicken. Bake at 350°F (180°C) 30 minutes; drain. In a small saucepan, combine soup mix, brown sugar, tomato sauce, water, vinegar and pineapple. Simmer, stirring constantly, until sauce is slightly thickened. Pour sauce over chicken and bake, basting occasionally, for 30 minutes or until chicken is tender.

Microwave: Prepare chicken and sauce as above. Heat sauce in a 2-cup (500 mL) glass measure. Brush half the sauce over chicken. Cover with waxed paper; heat at HIGH (100%) 10 minutes. Turn chicken over, brush with remaining sauce, heat at HIGH 8–10 minutes or until tender. Let stand, covered, 5 minutes.

Makes 6 servings.

Calories per serving: 617   Protein: Excellent   Iron and vitamin C: Good

CHICKEN INDIA

Preparation: about 10 minutes   Cook: about 50 minutes

If you've never tried curry with chicken, you'll be intrigued with this blending of flavors.

2½–3 lb	chicken, cut into serving pieces	1.25–1.5 kg
2 tbsp	vegetable oil	25 mL
1½ cups	water	375 mL
½ tsp	salt	2 mL
½ cup	milk	125 mL
1	package Lipton Pasta & Sauce — Creamy Garlic Raffaello	1
1 tsp	curry powder	5 mL
1	medium apple, sliced	1

In a large skillet, over medium-high heat, brown chicken in hot oil; drain. Add water and salt; simmer, covered, 40 minutes or until chicken is tender. Remove chicken and keep warm. Into skillet, add milk and bring to a boil; stir in pasta and sauce mix and curry. Continue cooking, uncovered, over medium heat, stirring occasionally, 8 minutes or until noodles are tender. Remove from heat. Let stand, covered, 3–5 minutes to allow sauce to thicken. To serve, arrange chicken over noodles; top with apple slices.

Microwave: In a 6-cup (1.5 L) covered casserole, heat oil at HIGH (100%) 1 minute. Add chicken, brown at HIGH 3–4 minutes; turn once. Add water and salt; heat, covered, at HIGH 12–15 minutes or until tender. Remove chicken and keep warm. Add milk; heat to a boil; stir in remaining ingredients. Heat, uncovered, at HIGH 5–6 minutes, stirring once. Let stand, covered, 5 minutes. Stir and serve with chicken.

Makes approximately 6 servings.

TIP: Take time to dry chicken pieces thoroughly before you put them in hot oil. Water added to hot fat will always cause splattering.

Calories per serving: 700   Protein: Excellent   Iron and riboflavin: Good

APRICOT ONION CHICKEN

Preparation: about 5 minutes   Cook: about 45 minutes

Whenever good cooks get together, they love to exchange their best recipes. This is one that is traded frequently.

3	whole chicken breasts, split, skinned, boned	3
1	pouch Lipton Onion Soup	1
⅓ cup	apricot jam	75 mL
1 cup	Russian salad dressing	250 mL

Place chicken in a shallow baking pan. Combine soup mix, jam and salad dressing. Pour half over chicken. Bake at 350°F (180°C) about 45 minutes; spoon glaze over chicken during baking.

Microwave: Arrange chicken in 12 × 8-inch (3 L) casserole. Combine soup mix, jam and salad dressing. Spread over chicken, covering each piece. Cover with waxed paper. Heat at HIGH (100%) 14–17 minutes; turn after 8 minutes. Let stand, covered, 5–10 minutes.

Makes 6 servings.

TIP: Remaining sauce may be used as a barbecue glaze on spareribs, chicken pieces, hamburgers, steaks or wieners.

Calories per serving: 422   Protein: Good

MEXICAN-STYLE CHICKEN DINNER

Preparation: about 20 minutes   Cook: about 50 minutes

This meal-in-a-dish can be refrigerated up to 24 hours before cooking. Just add 15 to 20 minutes to the normal cooking time. It can also be frozen.

6	chicken pieces	6
2 tbsp	vegetable oil	25 mL
1/2 cup	EACH: chopped onion, green pepper	125 mL
1	can (12 oz/341 mL) kernel corn	1
1	can (14 oz/398 mL) red kidney beans	1
1	pouch Lipton Chicken Rice Soup	1
1	can (7 1/2 oz/213 mL) tomato sauce	1
1/2 cup	water	125 mL
2–3 tsp	chili powder	10–15 mL
1/2 tsp	oregano	2 mL

In a medium skillet, over medium-high heat, brown chicken in hot oil. Remove and arrange in a greased oblong casserole or baking pan. Sauté onion in skillet until tender, but not brown. Add green pepper, corn, kidney beans, soup mix, tomato sauce, water and seasonings. Pour vegetable mixture over chicken pieces. Bake, uncovered, at 350°F (180°C) 40–50 minutes.

Microwave: In a medium casserole, brown chicken in oil at HIGH (100%) 5–6 minutes. Place in oblong dish. Heat onion in casserole 2 minutes. Add remaining ingredients. Pour over chicken. Cover with plastic wrap and heat at HIGH 10 minutes, stirring once. Heat 10 minutes longer or until tender. Let stand, covered, 5 minutes.

Makes 6 servings.

Calories per serving: 468   Fiber, vitamin C and iron: Excellent   Vitamin A and protein: Good

CHICKEN TACOS

Preparation: about 10 minutes   Cook: about 5 minutes

One of my daughters learned to make tacos in Grade 8 Home Economics class. Now in university, it's still among her favorite recipes for lunch or supper. She likes to serve tacos with a salad or Fiesta Rice (page 92).

2 cups	diced cooked chicken *or* turkey	500 mL
1/4 cup	chopped green onion	50 mL
2 tbsp	chopped green pepper	25 mL
2 tbsp	mayonnaise	25 mL
1/4 cup	grated Black Diamond Mild Cheddar Cheese	50 mL
1	package MexiCasa Taco Seasoning Mix	1
1	package MexiCasa Taco Shells (10)	1
	Shredded lettuce, chopped tomato, Mexicasa Taco Sauce *or* Taco Relish	

In a medium bowl, combine all ingredients with the seasoning mix. Arrange taco shells on a baking pan. Divide chicken filling between shells. Bake at 350°F (180°C) 5–7 minutes or until filling and shells are heated; or in a small saucepan, heat chicken filling until cheese melts and mixture is hot. Use to fill crisp taco shells. Garnish as desired with lettuce, tomatoes, taco sauce or taco relish.

Makes 10 tacos.

Calories per serving: 152, without garnishes

CHICKEN AUX FRAMBOISES

Preparation: about 15 minutes   Cook: about 25 minutes

This entrée will win you many accolades. It was developed in the Lipton Consumer Test Kitchens for an awards luncheon, held at a convention of the Canadian Home Economics Association.

4	boneless chicken breasts, skin removed	4
¼ cup	Becel Margarine, melted	50 mL
½ cup	finely chopped onion	125 mL
½ cup	EACH: raspberry vinegar, water	125 mL
1	OXO Chicken Bouillon Cube	1
1 tbsp	sugar	15 mL
¼ cup	tomato sauce	50 mL
½ cup	plain yogurt	125 mL
⅔ cup	fresh or frozen unsweetened raspberries	150 mL

Lightly flatten each chicken breast with a rolling pin. In a large skillet, over medium-high heat, sauté chicken breasts in margarine, 3–4 minutes on each side or until lightly browned. Remove from skillet, add onion, cover and cook over low heat until tender, about 10 minutes.

Add vinegar, water, bouillon cube, sugar and tomato sauce. Heat until bouillon cube is dissolved; add chicken. Cover and cook gently 10–15 minutes or until chicken is tender. Remove chicken to a heated serving platter. Rapidly cook remaining liquid until reduced and slightly thickened. Whisk in yogurt and add raspberries; heat but do not boil. Pour sauce over chicken and serve with white rice and a green vegetable.

Makes 4 servings.

TIPS: 1. If raspberry vinegar is unavailable, replace with white vinegar and add extra raspberries. 2. To prevent raspberries from breaking up, try to avoid stirring sauce after they are added.

Calories per serving: 289   Protein; vitamins A and C: Good

WESTERN CHICKEN SAUTÉ

Preparation: about 10 minutes   Cook: about 20 minutes

The faintly evergreen aroma and taste of rosemary lends emphasis to the fresh citrus tang of orange for a chicken dish inspired by West Coast cooks. The use of herbs and orange juice eliminates the need for salt in this recipe.

2	whole chicken breasts, split, skinned, boned	2
2 tbsp	all-purpose flour	25 mL
¼ cup	Becel Margarine, melted	50 mL
¾ cup	orange juice	175 mL
1 tbsp	red wine vinegar	15 mL
½ tsp	dried leaf rosemary, crumbled	2 mL
¼ tsp	grated orange peel	1 mL
2 tbsp	chopped fresh parsley	25 mL
1	orange, peeled and sectioned	1

Pound chicken slightly to flatten to an even thickness. Dredge in flour, shaking off excess; reserve flour. In a large skillet, over medium-high heat, sauté chicken in margarine until golden brown on both sides. Remove and keep warm. Stir flour, orange juice, vinegar, rosemary and orange peel into skillet. Return chicken to skillet; cover and simmer 15–20 minutes or until tender, stirring occasionally. Sprinkle with parsley and garnish with orange sections.

Microwave: In a shallow covered casserole, melt margarine at HIGH (100%) 45–60 seconds. Brown prepared chicken, covered, at HIGH 5 minutes; turn part way through. Remove and keep warm. Stir flour, orange juice, vinegar, rosemary and orange peel into dish. Heat at HIGH 2–3 minutes until thickened, stirring frequently. Return chicken, cover and heat at HIGH 7–8 minutes or until tender. Let stand, covered, 5 minutes.

Makes 4 servings.

Calories per serving: 279   Vitamin C: Excellent   Vitamin A: Good

JEWELED CHICKEN

Preparation: about 10 minutes   Cook: about 40 minutes

Often food is so attractive it needs a special name. Imagine a sauce of emeralds, pearls and rubies when you look at the colorful green peas, white onions and red pimientos used in the sauce for this recipe.

3	medium, whole chicken breasts, split, skinned, boned	3
¼ cup	Becel Margarine, divided	50 mL
2 tbsp	all-purpose flour	25 mL
1 cup	skim milk	250 mL
1	OXO Chicken Bouillon Cube	1
¼ tsp	freshly ground black pepper	1 mL
¼ cup	dry vermouth *or* white wine	50 mL
1	medium onion, quartered	1
½ cup	pimiento strips, drained	125 mL
½ cup	frozen peas	125 mL

In a large skillet, over medium-high heat, brown chicken breasts in 2 tbsp (25 mL) melted margarine. Remove and arrange in a shallow baking dish. In same skillet, melt remaining margarine. Stir in flour and cook 1 minute. Gradually stir in milk, bouillon cube and pepper. Cook, stirring constantly, until sauce boils and thickens; add vermouth, onion and pimiento. Spoon sauce over chicken. Bake at 350°F (180°C) 30–40 minutes or until chicken tests done. Add peas during last 10 minutes.

Microwave: In a shallow casserole, melt 2 tbsp (25 mL) margarine at HIGH (100%) 45–60 seconds. Brown chicken at HIGH 5–7 minutes; turn part way through; remove. Melt remaining margarine, stir in flour, heat at HIGH and stir for 30 seconds. Gradually stir in milk, bouillon cube and pepper. Heat at HIGH 3–4 minutes; stir once. Add remaining ingredients. Return chicken, cover with plastic wrap; heat at HIGH 6–8 minutes.

Makes 6 servings.

Calories per serving: 250   Protein; vitamins A and C: Good

TURKEY PRIMAVERA ALFREDO

Preparation: about 5 minutes   Cook: about 10 minutes

Look no further. Here is a recipe to use up that leftover cooked poultry.

1 cup	water	250 mL
1 cup	milk	250 mL
2 tbsp	margarine *or* butter	25 mL
1	package Lipton Pasta & Sauce — Fettucine Alfredo	1
1 cup	thinly sliced zucchini	250 mL
2 cups	diced cooked turkey *or* chicken	500 mL
1	medium tomato, diced	1

In a medium saucepan, bring water, milk and margarine to a boil. Stir in pasta and sauce mix and zucchini. Simmer over medium heat 5 minutes, stirring occasionally. Add turkey and tomato. Cook and stir for 3 minutes; let stand, covered, 3–5 minutes to allow sauce to thicken. Stir and serve.

Microwave: In a 6-cup (1.5 L) covered casserole, bring water, milk and margarine to a boil at HIGH (100%). Stir in pasta and sauce mix and zucchini. Heat, uncovered, at HIGH 3 minutes, stirring once. Add turkey and tomato; heat at HIGH 3 minutes. Let stand, covered, 5 minutes. Stir and serve.

Makes 4 servings.

Calories per serving: 337   Iron; vitamins A and C: Good

CHICKEN OR TURKEY MOLE

Preparation: about 30 minutes   Cook: 1 hour, 30 minutes

This is a traditional Mexican dish served on Christmas Eve as well as throughout the year. The rich mole sauce contains chocolate and peanut butter, which are interesting flavors to combine with the chili seasoning. Ensalada de Noche Buena (page 32) is a must with this famous recipe.

4 cups	water	1 L
1 tbsp	Lawry's Seasoned Salt	15 mL
2½–3 lb	broiler-fryer chicken *or* turkey, cut up	1.25–1.5 kg
1	small onion, finely chopped	1
2 tbsp	vegetable oil	25 mL
1	can (14 oz/398 mL) tomatoes, undrained	1
1	package MexiCasa Chili Seasoning Mix	1
1½ cups	chicken broth	375 mL
¼ cup	chunky-style peanut butter	50 mL
2	squares unsweetened Mexican chocolate, grated	2
2 tsp	sesame seeds, toasted	10 mL

In a deep saucepan or Dutch oven, combine water, salt and chicken. Bring to a boil, then reduce heat, cover and simmer about 45 minutes or until tender. Save broth to use in mole sauce. Meanwhile, in a large skillet, sauté onion in hot oil. Add tomatoes and chili seasoning mix. Combine thoroughly, breaking up tomatoes with a spoon. Add chicken broth and bring to a boil. Add peanut butter and chocolate; stir thoroughly. Reduce heat and simmer, uncovered, 15 minutes, stirring occasionally. Place chicken in a large shallow casserole. Pour mole sauce over chicken. Bake at 350°F (180°C) 20–30 minutes. Sprinkle with toasted sesame seeds. May be frozen.

Makes 4–6 servings.

TIPS: 1. Turkey parts may be substituted for chicken. If this is done, remove turkey meat from bone after simmering and cut into cubes. Use turkey broth. 2. Mexican chocolate may be substituted with 2 squares semi-sweet chocolate, 2 tbsp (25 mL) sugar and ¼ tsp (1 mL) cinnamon. 3. Recipe may be made ahead and baked just before serving or baked ahead and reheated.

Calories per serving: 747   Iron and protein: Excellent   Vitamins A and C; riboflavin: Good

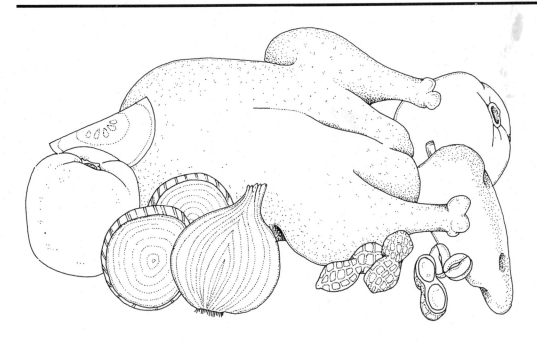

FISH AND SEAFOOD

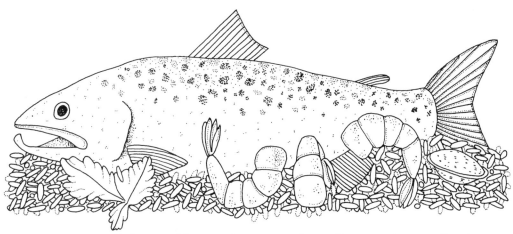

The consumption of fish could soon rise as much as 90 percent according to recent government research studies. Besides its economy, fish is prized for its ease of preparation and fast cooking. (The Canadian Department of Fisheries recommends cooking fish ten minutes per inch (2.5 cm) of thickness at 400°F (200°C). Be sure not to overcook or it will fall apart when it is served.) As well, fish is a nutritious addition to any meal. Recent medical findings have reported the discovery of Omega-3 in certain fish and shellfish living in colder salt and fresh waters. Omega-3 is a fatty acid which lowers cholesterol levels and prevents blood clotting, both common causes of heart disease. Fish is no longer just brain food but heart food, too.

QUICK SEASONING TIPS

Fish can be quickly prepared by the shortcut cook and quickly varied with herb spreads. These spreads are made with butter, margarine or a combination of both. Blend thoroughly: ½ cup (125 mL) butter, 1 tbsp (15 mL) lemon juice, 3 tbsp (45 mL) finely chopped fresh herbs and ¼ tsp (1 mL) each: salt and pepper. This preparation can be stored up to two weeks in the refrigerator. Another excellent choice is dill butter or *fines herbes* butter. Instead of using one type of herb, combine 1 tbsp (15 mL) each: minced parsley and chopped chives with ½ tsp (2 mL) each: tarragon and chervil leaves.

CREATIVE GARNISHING TIPS

Fish lends itself particularly well to garnishing. Arrange a whole fish on a bed of curly endive and lemon twists. Or use dark green parsley with lighter green grapes and golden slivered almonds.

You don't have to serve fish with lemon. For fish fillets, citrus garnishes such as spirals of orange or lime peel are an interesting change. Try black olives and cherry tomatoes with watercress. Use lime twists or small bunches of purple grapes with salmon steaks.

With shellfish, individual serving dishes, such as scallop dishes for Scallops in Wine (page 82), are attractive. Garnish with buttered bread crumbs and cheese. If you're serving Scampi Dijon (page 81), buy a few extra large shrimp for garnishes.

CITRUS SALMON STEAKS

Preparation: about 10 minutes   Marinate: 6–12 hours   Cook: about 20 minutes

The tang of lime contrasts with the richness of salmon while ginger lends a subtle contrast to this barbecue specialty.

4–6	salmon steaks	4–6
	Juice of 2 limes	
1/4 cup	dry sherry	50 mL
1 tbsp	minced fresh ginger	15 mL
2 tsp	soy sauce	10 mL
1/4 cup	melted Becel Margarine	50 mL

Place salmon steaks in a shallow baking dish. In a small bowl, combine lime juice, sherry, ginger and soy sauce; pour over salmon. Marinate, covered, 6–12 hours in refrigerator. Drain marinade and reserve. Place salmon steaks on barbecue grill; add margarine to marinade and use to baste fish; grill about 10 minutes per side.

Makes 4–6 servings.

TIPS: 1. For uniform cooking, all seafood and meat should be an even thickness. 2. Marinades add flavor and keep food moist.

Calories per serving: 337   Calcium and protein: Good

PACIFIC MOUSSE

Preparation: about 10 minutes   Chill: 4 hours

The velvety texture of this mousse will make it a favorite for your entertaining. Serve as an appetizer with melba toast. Or try it with black bread — the robust flavor of the bread balances the delicate taste of the salmon.

1	pouch Knox Unflavoured Gelatine	1
1/4 cup	cold water	50 mL
1/2 cup	EACH: boiling water, mayonnaise	125 mL
1 tbsp	EACH: lemon juice, finely grated onion	15 mL
1/8 tsp	Tabasco sauce	0.5 mL
1/2 tsp	dry mustard	2 mL
1 tsp	EACH: salt, dill weed	5 mL
1	can (7 1/2 oz/213 g) salmon, drained, finely flaked	1
	Watercress	

In a large bowl, soften gelatine in cold water. Add boiling water; stir until gelatine is completely dissolved. Cool to room temperature. Stir in mayonnaise, lemon juice, onion, Tabasco sauce, mustard, salt and dill. Refrigerate about 20 minutes or until mixture begins to thicken slightly. Fold in flaked salmon; place in a small lightly greased loaf pan or 2-cup (500 mL) mold. Cover and chill for at least 4 hours. Unmold and serve garnished with watercress.

Makes 6 servings.

Calories per serving: 206

CREAMY MUSHROOM FISH CASSEROLE

Preparation: about 10 minutes   Cook: 45 minutes

This creamy casserole of green broccoli and white fish fillets served with sliced tomatoes is a quick colorful supper. For variety, you can substitute tuna, salmon, shrimp, ham or chicken.

1/2 cup	EACH: chopped celery, onion, uncooked rice	125 mL
2 tbsp	margarine *or* butter, melted	25 mL
1	pouch Lipton Onion-Mushroom Soup	1
1 1/2 cups	milk	375 mL
1	package (300 g) frozen, chopped broccoli, thawed and drained	1
1 lb	fish fillets	500 g

In a skillet, sauté celery, onion and rice in margarine, about 5 minutes. Add soup mix and milk. Cook until thickened, about 5 minutes. Add broccoli. Arrange fish in a greased shallow baking pan. Top with broccoli mixture. Bake, covered, at 350°F (180°C) 20 minutes; uncover, bake 15 minutes.

Microwave: In a 6-cup (1.5 L) casserole, melt margarine at HIGH (100%) 45 seconds. Add celery, onion and rice; heat at HIGH 3–4 minutes. Add soup mix and milk. Heat at HIGH 2–3 minutes until thickened, stirring frequently. Add broccoli. Prepare casserole as above. Cover and cook at HIGH 10–12 minutes. Let stand 5 minutes.

Makes 3–4 servings.

TIP: Thaw wrapped frozen fish in the refrigerator to preserve delicious juices. Never refreeze fish once it has thawed.

Calories per serving: 302   Fiber; vitamins A and C: Good   Calcium, protein and iron: Good

SEAFOOD MARINADE

Preparation: about 5 minutes   Marinate: 2–4 hours   Cook: about 6 minutes

I've used this barbecue marinade for many types of seafood and whole or filleted fish. Each time I enjoy it more. The easiest way to barbecue fish is with a fish basket. This eliminates the difficulty of turning it on the grill. If a basket is unavailable, puncture holes in a large sheet of greased heavy-duty aluminum foil. Arrange fish on foil and place on barbecue rack. To develop the customary barbecued smoked flavor, do not wrap the fish with the foil. Instead cover with a loose tent of foil or the barbecue cover.

1/2 cup	vegetable oil	125 mL
2 tbsp	soy sauce	25 mL
1 tbsp	Lawry's Garlic Powder	15 mL
1 tsp	salt	5 mL
1/4 tsp	Lawry's Seasoned Pepper	1 mL
1/4 cup	rye whisky	50 mL
2 tsp	brown sugar	10 mL
2–3 lb	fish fillets (e.g. salmon, sole, halibut, haddock)	1–1.5 kg

In a small bowl, combine all ingredients for marinade. Pour over fish and leave to marinate, covered, 2–4 hours in refrigerator. Place on grill and barbecue 3–4 minutes per side, just until fish flakes, brushing with marinade several times during cooking.

Makes 6–8 servings.

Calories per serving: 472   Vitamin A: Excellent   Protein: Good

MIXED SEAFOOD BROCHETTE

Preparation: about 10 minutes   Marinate: 3 hours   Cook: about 10 minutes

These marinated seafood brochettes can be barbecued or broiled in five to seven minutes. For a complete meal, thread cubed zucchini, red pepper and pineapple alternately on the skewers with the fish.

3 lb	mixed seafood and fish, (e.g. haddock, cod, sea bass, swordfish, shrimp, scallops)	1.5 kg
2	cloves garlic	2
½ tsp	Lawry's Seasoned Salt	2 mL
½ cup	EACH: olive oil, lemon juice	125 mL
¼ cup	EACH: soy sauce, minced parsley	50 mL
2 tbsp	finely chopped onion	25 mL
½ tsp	pepper	2 mL
	Hot cooked rice	

Cut all fish into small cubes and arrange in a shallow glass dish. Shell and devein shrimp, leaving tails on. In a food processor, combine garlic and seasoned salt; let machine run until garlic is finely minced. Add remaining ingredients, except rice, and process until well mixed. Pour over seafood. Marinate, covered, 3 hours in refrigerator. Drain marinade, thread seafood on skewers; broil or barbecue, 5–7 minutes on each side; baste and turn frequently. Serve on a bed of rice.

Makes 6 servings.

Calories per serving: 381, without rice   Iron, protein, thiamin and vitamin C: Good

POACHED FISH FILLETS WITH FRESH LEMON SAUCE

Preparation: about 10 minutes   Cook: about 10 minutes

Don't forget to serve fish when you're considering food that is low in calories and saturated fat. It's a perfect choice for any meal.

1½ cups	sliced onion	375 mL
1 cup	diagonally sliced carrots	250 mL
3 tbsp	Becel Margarine, melted	45 mL
1 lb	flounder or sole fillets	500 g
1¼ cups	water	300 mL
¼ tsp	EACH: salt, pepper	1 mL
3 tbsp	fresh lemon juice	45 mL
1 tbsp	cornstarch	15 mL
2 tbsp	water	25 mL
2 tbsp	chopped fresh dill or parsley	25 mL

In a large skillet, cook onion and carrots in margarine 5–7 minutes or until tender-crisp. Fold fillets in thirds; arrange in skillet over vegetables. Add water, salt and pepper. Cover and cook 4–5 minutes or until fish flakes easily when tested with a fork. With a slotted spoon or spatula, remove fish and vegetables to a heated serving platter. Measure 1¼ cups (300 mL) stock, reserve remainder. Return stock to skillet, add lemon juice; stir cornstarch into 2 tbsp (25 mL) reserved stock; stir into skillet. Bring to a boil for 1 minute. Pour sauce over fish and vegetables. Sprinkle with dill.

Makes 4 servings.

TIP: Notice a fishy smell at your house for days after you poach fish? Next time, use a drop of vinegar in the cooking liquid.

Calories per serving: 374   Vitamin A: Excellent   Iron, protein and vitamin C: Good

FISHERMAN'S STEW

Preparation: about 10 minutes   Cook: about 15 minutes

With this hearty soup, similar to French Bouillabaisse, you need only crusty bread and a crisp salad for an enjoyable lunch or supper.

½	small green pepper, chopped	½
2	cloves garlic, minced	2
2 tbsp	olive oil	25 mL
1	can (19 oz/540 mL) tomatoes, undrained	1
1	can (5 oz/142 mL) clams, drained (reserve liquid)	1
½ cup	dry white wine	125 mL
1	pouch Lipton Bon Appétit Farmhouse Chicken Vegetable Soup	1
1 tsp	basil	5 mL
½ lb	haddock *or* halibut fillets, cut into serving pieces	250 g
1	can (4 oz/113 g) large shrimp	1
1 tbsp	chopped fresh parsley	15 mL

In a medium saucepan, cook green pepper and garlic in hot oil 2–3 minutes. Add tomatoes, clam liquid, wine, soup mix, basil and fish. Cover and simmer 8–10 minutes. Add shrimp, parsley and drained clams. Cook 4–5 minutes or until heated.

Microwave: In an 8-cup (2 L) covered casserole, cook green pepper and garlic in oil at HIGH (100%) 2 minutes. Add tomatoes, clam liquid, wine, soup mix, basil and fish. Heat, covered, at HIGH 6–8 minutes. Add remaining ingredients. Heat 2–3 minutes. Let stand 5 minutes.

Makes 4 servings.

Calories per serving: 319   Iron, protein and vitamin C: Excellent   Vitamin A: Good

FLOUNDER AND MUSHROOMS EN PAPILLOTE

Preparation: about 10 minutes   Cook: about 20 minutes

Using aluminum foil, you can easily duplicate the French method of cooking food in greaseproof paper, called *en papillote*. This retains the moistness and aroma of the food. You will be treated to a tantalizing fragrance when you open the foil package at the table.

1 tbsp	green onion, chopped	15 mL
2 tbsp	Becel Margarine, melted	25 mL
½ lb	fresh mushrooms, chopped	250 g
3 tbsp	dry white wine	45 mL
1 tbsp	EACH: lemon juice, chopped fresh parsley	15 mL
4	flounder fillets	4
	Freshly ground black pepper	

In a medium skillet, over medium-high heat, sauté green onion in margarine until soft; add mushrooms and cook 3 minutes. Add wine, lemon juice and parsley; cook until most of the liquid evaporates, about 3 minutes. Lightly grease 4 pieces of heavy-duty foil with margarine. Place a fish fillet on each piece; season with pepper. Top with mushroom sauce. Draw edges of foil together and seal. Bake at 400°F (200°C) 20 minutes or until fish flakes.

Makes 4 servings.

Calories per serving: 186

FISH FILLETS THERMIDOR

Preparation: about 15 minutes   Cook: about 15 minutes

An adaptation of Lobster Thermidor, this recipe substitutes economical fillets for lobster. The smooth cheese sauce uses fish liquor and skim milk instead of heavy cream to reduce the saturated fat.

¼ cup	Becel Margarine, divided	50 mL
1 tsp	Dijon mustard	5 mL
4	fish fillets (e.g. sole or flounder—about 1 lb/500g)	4
	Freshly ground black pepper	
¾ cup	skim milk, divided	175 mL
1 cup	fresh mushrooms, thinly sliced	250 mL
4 tsp	all-purpose flour	20 mL
½ cup	grated Swiss cheese	125 mL
2 tbsp	dry sherry	25 mL

In a small saucepan, heat 1 tbsp (15 mL) margarine and mustard; brush over fish fillets. Season with pepper. Roll fillets and place in an 8-inch (2 L) square baking dish. Brush with 1 tbsp (15 mL) milk. Bake at 400°F (200°C) 10–15 minutes or until fish flakes easily with a fork. In a small saucepan, sauté mushrooms in 1 tbsp (15 mL) melted margarine for 1 minute. Remove mushrooms. In same saucepan, melt remaining margarine; stir in flour; cook 1 minute. Gradually stir in remaining milk; bring to a boil. Add cheese and sherry; stir until cheese melts. Remove fillets from oven; drain liquid and stir into sauce. Add mushrooms; spoon sauce over fish. Broil 1–2 minutes until sauce is lightly browned.

Makes 4 servings.

Calories per serving: 332   Calcium: Excellent   Vitamin A and protein: Good

BAKED SNAPPER WITH NUTTY RICE STUFFING

Preparation: about 15 minutes   Cook: about 20 minutes

To enhance the delicate taste of snapper, garnish the fish with orange slices and fresh herbs and serve it with a cucumber and melon salad.

1	small onion, chopped	1
1	clove garlic, crushed	1
2 tbsp	Becel Margarine, melted	25 mL
½ cup	quick cook rice	125 mL
¾ cup	water	175 mL
1	OXO Chicken Bouillon Cube	1
	Grated peel of 1 orange	
1 tbsp	EACH: raisins, toasted slivered almonds	15 mL
3 lb	snapper, cleaned and scaled	1.5 kg
2 tbsp	orange juice	25 mL
	Lawry's Seasoned Pepper	

In a small skillet, over low heat, sauté onion and garlic in margarine until soft. Stir in rice, water, bouillon cube and orange peel; bring to a boil, cover and simmer 5–8 minutes or until rice is tender and liquid is absorbed. Remove from heat, stir in raisins and almonds. Arrange fish on a large piece of greased foil. Spoon rice mixture into fish cavity; secure with skewers. Pour orange juice over fish; season with pepper. Draw edges of foil together and seal. Bake at 400°F (200°C) 20–25 minutes or until fish flakes easily with a fork.

Makes 6 servings.

TIP: A cheese slicer makes an excellent fish scaler. Just run the wire against the grain of the scales from the tail to the head.

Calories per serving: 284   Iron, protein and thiamin: Good

SPAGHETTI WITH SEAFOOD SAUCE

Preparation: about 10 minutes   Cook: about 10 minutes

An Italian neighbor first treated me to spaghetti served with seafood sauce. It was one of the many dishes she served at a luncheon and everyone loved it. Try this seafood version, made with mussels and crabmeat.

1 lb	fish fillets (e.g. perch, snapper or grouper) cut into small cubes	500 g
2 tbsp	Becel Margarine, melted	25 mL
1	large green pepper, chopped	1
3	large tomatoes, seeded and chopped	3
½ cup	EACH: tomato paste, dry white wine	125 mL
1 tsp	dried oregano	5 mL
1 lb	mussels, washed, cooked and removed from shell	500 g
1	medium can crabmeat, flaked	1
	Lawry's Seasoned Pepper	
¾ lb	cooked whole wheat spaghetti or enriched pasta	375 g

In a large skillet, over medium heat, cook fish in margarine for 1 minute. Add green pepper, tomatoes, tomato paste, wine and oregano; bring to a boil, reduce heat and simmer 10 minutes, stirring occasionally. Add mussels and crabmeat, cook for 2–3 minutes, sprinkle with seasoned pepper and serve over spaghetti.

Microwave: In a large oblong dish, melt margarine at HIGH (100%) 30 seconds. Add fish, green pepper, tomatoes, tomato paste, wine and oregano. Heat, covered, at HIGH 5–6 minutes. Add mussels and crabmeat; heat at HIGH 1–2 minutes. Let stand, covered, 5 minutes. Sprinkle with seasoned pepper.

Makes 6 servings.

Calories per serving: 490   Iron; vitamins A and C; thiamin: Excellent   Protein: Good

SCAMPI DIJON

Preparation: about 3 minutes   Cook: about 10 minutes

If you like collecting recipes from famous restaurants, you'll enjoy this Chef's specialty from The Westside Broiler. It is one of Lawry's Los Angeles restaurants.

2	cloves garlic, finely minced	2
½ cup	margarine or butter, melted	125 mL
10	raw shrimp, peeled	10
2 tsp	EACH: dry vermouth, lemon juice, Dijon mustard	10 mL
½ tsp	chopped fresh parsley	2 mL
¼ tsp	Lawry's Seasoned Salt	1 mL

In a medium skillet, over medium-high heat, sauté garlic in margarine until tender, about

3 minutes. Add shrimp and cook until pink, about 5 minutes. Add remaining ingredients; warm through over low heat.

Microwave: In a casserole, melt margarine at HIGH (100%) 1 minute. Add garlic, heat at HIGH 1 minute; add shrimp, heat at HIGH 3–4 minutes. Add remaining ingredients, heat on MEDIUM (50%).

Makes 2 servings.

Calories per serving: 680   Vitamin A and iron: Excellent   Calcium and protein: Good

SHRIMP ASPARAGUS FETTUCINE

Preparation: about 10 minutes   Cook: about 10 minutes

It seems hard to believe that this attractive shortcut pasta dish, prepared in minutes, could be such a taste treat. Perfect for the after-five host or hostess.

1½ cups	water	350 mL
½ cup	milk	125 mL
2 tbsp	margarine *or* butter	25 mL
1	package Lipton Pasta & Sauce — Fettucine Alfredo	1
1	package (300 g) frozen asparagus spears	1
½ tsp	basil	2 mL
½ lb	uncooked shrimp, cleaned	250 g

In a large saucepan, bring water, milk and margarine to a boil. Stir in pasta and sauce mix, asparagus and basil. Simmer, over medium heat, stirring occasionally, 4 minutes. Add shrimp and cook, stirring occasionally, for an additional 4 minutes or until pasta and shrimp are tender. Remove from heat. Let stand, covered, 3–5 minutes to allow sauce to thicken.

Microwave: In a 6-cup (1.5 L) covered casserole, bring water, milk and margarine to a boil at HIGH (100%). Stir in pasta and sauce mix, asparagus and basil. Heat, uncovered, at HIGH 5–6 minutes, stirring once. Add shrimp; heat at HIGH 4 minutes or until pasta and shrimp are tender. Let stand, covered, 5 minutes to allow sauce to thicken. Stir and serve.

Makes 2–3 servings.

TIP: Fresh asparagus may be used but must be cooked first.

Calories per serving: 360   Vitamins A and C: Excellent   Calcium and iron: Good

SCALLOPS IN WINE

Preparation: 5 minutes   Marinate: about 15 minutes   Cook: about 5 minutes

For a gourmet meal, try this simple scallop recipe. It is instant elegance!

1 tbsp	Becel Margarine	15 mL
¼ cup	dry white wine	50 mL
	Juice of 1 lemon	
½ tsp	thyme	2 mL
1 lb	scallops	500 g

In a medium saucepan, heat margarine, wine, lemon juice and thyme. Pour over rinsed scallops. Marinate 15-20 minutes at room temperature. Bake at 450°F (230°C) 5–6 minutes. Do not overcook.

Microwave: Marinate scallops as above. Heat, covered, at HIGH (100%) 3–4 minutes. Let stand 5 minutes.

Makes 4 servings.

Calories per serving: 180   Iron and protein: Good

GOURMET SEAFOOD TACOS

Preparation: about 10 minutes   Cook: 5 minutes

Serve this cold seafood variation for a "fun food" at your next informal party. Put out bowls of filling and garnishes and let your guests make their own. An easy way to entertain!

1	medium can tuna, crabmeat *or* salmon, drained and flaked		1
2 tbsp	finely chopped fresh parsley	25 mL	
1 tsp	lemon juice	5 mL	
¼ cup	finely chopped celery	50 mL	
2 tbsp	finely chopped onion	25 mL	
2 tbsp	MexiCasa Taco Relish	25 mL	
⅓ cup	mayonnaise	75 mL	
1	package MexiCasa Taco Shells (10) Grated Black Diamond Cheddar Cheese, shredded lettuce, chopped tomato		1

In a small bowl, combine tuna, parsley, lemon juice, celery, onion, relish and mayonnaise. Heat taco shells according to package directions. Spoon filling into taco shells; garnish with cheese, lettuce and tomato.

Makes approximately 1 cup (250 mL) — sufficient filling for 10 tacos.

Calories per taco: 142, without garnishes

POTATOES, RICE AND PASTA

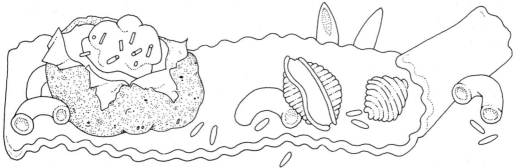

One of my friend's mothers always had room for one more at the table. Whenever there was a last-minute guest for supper, she'd cheerfully say, "I'll throw another potato in the pot." Certainly potatoes have always been known for their economy and versatility. They can even be served at brunch or breakfast. Potato and Mushroom Medley (page 93) is a good example. A part of most evening meals, they are one of the important sources of carbohydrates in the diet. Although they have a reputation as a high-calorie food, potatoes are low in calories. It is the toppings used with them that add calories. Rice and pasta are two other important economical and nutritious sources for meal planning. This section's recipes suggest a variety of delicious ways to use them.

QUICK SEASONING TIPS

It's easy to add a fresh taste to your cooking when you freeze the herbs grown in your garden. Wash the herbs and dry them well with a salad spinner or paper towels. Spread the leaves loosely on a baking sheet, place in the freezer and then package them in plastic bags. Freezing retains the color and flavor of herbs, but they lose their crisp quality. Use them in your cooking, before defrosting, in the same proportions as fresh herbs. They are not appropriate for garnishing.

CREATIVE GARNISHING TIPS

Use these low-calorie garnishes and seasonings for potatoes. Sprinkle on some sesame seeds or a mixture of dried herbs — parsley, chives, basil and dill. Top with tomato and grated cheese or chopped onion with coarsely grated black pepper. Drizzle on margarine or butter, thinned with lemon juice. Make up mock sour cream by blending cottage cheese and lemon juice in the blender. Try yogurt with mixed chives. Be creative with calories.

Because rice is bland, it needs colorful garnishes. Toss in chopped red and green peppers, chives, parsley, crumbled bacon or diced ham. Mold it into a ring and fill the center with bright stir-fried vegetables. Or fill the ring with snow peas and mushrooms and use cherry tomatoes as a garnish.

Pasta comes in hundreds of varieties. It is becoming more popular in cooking because it is quickly prepared and combines well with many foods. It needs only simple garnishes — a sprinkling of Parmesan cheese on spaghetti sauce, a sprig of basil on a square of lasagna.

MINUTE MEALS

When you have only minutes to cook, check these simple charts and the leftovers in your refrigerator. Then serve a Minute Meal your family will enjoy from your shortcut shelf.

1½ cups	water	375 mL*
½ cup	milk	125 mL
2 tbsp	margarine *or* butter	25 mL
	Lipton Noodles & Sauce, Vegetables, Meat and Helpful Extras	

Makes approximately 4 servings.

In a large saucepan, bring water, milk and margarine to a boil; stir in noodles and sauce mix and Step 1 ingredients. Simmer, uncovered, over medium heat for 5 minutes; stir occasionally. Stir in the remaining ingredients, Step 2 and Helpful Extras, if desired. Cook an additional 3 minutes or until noodles are tender. Let stand, covered, 3–5 minutes to allow sauce to thicken. *For Chicken and Butter & Herb flavors, increase water to 2 cups (500 mL); omit milk.

DISH	NOODLES & SAUCE	STEP 1	STEP 2	HELPFUL EXTRAS
Calico Noodle Supper	1 package Lipton Noodles & Sauce — Chicken	1 package (300 g) frozen mixed vegetables, partially thawed	2 cups (500 mL) cubed cooked ham	¼ cup (50 mL) raisins
Tantalizing Turkey Divan	1 package Lipton Noodles & Sauce — Creamy Parmesan	2 cups (500 mL) frozen broccoli florets	2 cups (500 mL) cut-up cooked turkey	¼ cup (50 mL) dry sherry
Pork 'n Beans Medley	1 package Lipton Noodles & Sauce — Sour Cream & Chives	1 package (300 g) frozen green beans, or peas, partially thawed	2 cups (500 mL) thinly sliced cooked pork	2 tbsp (25 mL) chopped pimiento
Easy Beef Stroganoff	1 package Lipton Noodles & Sauce — Stroganoff	1 cup (250 mL) mushrooms, ¼ cup (50 mL) diced onion	2 cups (500 mL) thinly sliced cooked beef	1 tsp (5 mL) poppy seeds (sprinkle over)
Herbed Seafood and Noodles	1 package Lipton Noodles & Sauce — Butter & Herb	1 package (300 g) frozen chopped asparagus, partially thawed	2 cups (500 mL) cooked fish fillet or shrimp	¼ cup (50 mL) slivered almonds (sprinkle over)

MAKE A SIDE DISH A MEAL

1 cup	water	250 mL*
1 cup	milk	250 mL
2 tbsp	margarine *or* butter	25 mL
	Lipton Pasta & Sauce, Vegetables, Meats and Helpful Extras	

*For Tomato & Herb Marinara, increase water to 2 cups (500 mL); omit milk.

In a large saucepan, bring water, milk and margarine to a boil; stir in pasta and sauce mix and Step 1 ingredients. Simmer, uncovered, over medium heat for 5 minutes; stir occasionally. Stir in the remaining ingredients, Step 2, and Helpful Extras, if desired. Cook an additional 3 minutes or until pasta is tender. Let stand, covered, 3–5 minutes to allow sauce to thicken.

Makes approximately 4 servings.

DISH	PASTA & SAUCE	STEP 1	STEP 2	HELPFUL EXTRAS
Beef Bourguignonne	1 package Lipton Pasta & Sauce — Creamy Bacon Carbonara	½ cup (125 mL) thinly sliced carrots, ¼ cup (50 mL) thinly sliced onions	2 cups (500 mL) cubed cooked beef, 1 cup (250 mL) sliced mushrooms	Replace ¼ cup (50 mL) water with red wine.
Spanish Skillet Noodles	1 package Lipton Pasta & Sauce — Tomato & Herb Marinara	2 tsp (10 mL) chili powder, ¼ cup (50 mL) diced green pepper	1 can (12 oz/341 mL) corn kernels, ¾ lb (375 g) browned ground beef, ⅔ cup (150 mL) grated Black Diamond Cheddar Cheese	Replace ½ cup (125 mL) milk with water. Sprinkle over ⅓ cup (75 mL) grated Black Diamond Cheddar Cheese.
Creamy Country Ham Pasta	1 package Lipton Pasta & Sauce — Creamy Garlic Raffaello	¼ cup (50 mL) chopped celery	2 cups (500 mL) cubed cooked ham, 2 tbsp (25 mL) coarsely chopped dried apricots, ½ cup (125 mL) snow peas, blanched	Replace ¼ cup (50 mL) water with dry sherry or white wine.

RICE AND SAUCE SUPPERS

2 cups	**water**	**500 mL**
1 tbsp	**margarine _or_ butter**	**15 mL**
	Lipton Rice & Sauce, Vegetables, Meats and Helpful Extras	

In a large saucepan, bring water, margarine, rice and sauce mix and Step 1 ingredients to a boil. Simmer, uncovered, over medium heat for 5 minutes; stir occasionally. Stir in the remaining ingredients, Step 2 and Helpful Extras, if desired. Cook an additional 5 minutes or until rice is tender.

Makes approximately 4 servings.

DISH	RICE & SAUCE	STEP 1	STEP 2	HELPFUL EXTRAS
Seafood Lime Pilaf	1 package Lipton Rice & Sauce — Pilaf	2 tbsp (25 mL) fresh lime juice	1 medium red pepper, cut into thin strips; 4 green onions, sliced; 1 regular size can salmon, shrimp or crab	Reduce water to 1⅔ cups (400 mL)
Frankly Delicious Dinner	1 package Lipton Rice & Sauce — Italian Tomato	6 wieners, diagonally sliced; 2 cups (500 mL) broccoli florets	½ cup (125 mL) corn kernels; 1 cup (250 mL) grated Black Diamond Cheddar Cheese	
Polynesian Rice and Pork	1 package Lipton Rice & Sauce — Polynesian	½ cup (125 mL) thinly sliced celery; ½ tsp (2 mL) cinnamon; ¼ tsp (1 mL) ground cloves	2 cups (500 mL) cut-up cooked pork; ½ green pepper, cut into strips; 1 can (10 oz/341 mL) mandarin oranges, drained	Replace ½ cup (125 mL) water with orange juice
Fast 'n Fancy Chicken	1 package Lipton Rice & Sauce—Harvest Chicken	½ cup (125 mL) EACH: thinly sliced carrots, celery, and onion; ¼ tsp (1 mL) pepper	2 cups (500 mL) cut-up cooked chicken; 1 green pepper, diced	May be prepared in a 6-cup (1.5 L) casserole, covered with pastry and baked at 425°F (220°C) for 20 minutes.

FETTUCINE VERDE

Preparation: 10 minutes   Cook: 3–8 minutes

Although *verde* means "green" in Italian, there's no reason not to use multi-colored pasta. Many more shapes and colors are available in today's grocery stores. Combine tomato and plain fettucine with spinach pasta for an Italian-flag meal.

1 cup	low-fat cottage cheese	250 mL
2 tbsp	Black Diamond Grated Parmesan Cheese	25 mL
2 tbsp	skim milk	25 mL
½ lb	spinach fettucine	250 g
2 tbsp	Becel Margarine	25 mL
	Freshly ground pepper	

In a blender or food processor, blend cottage cheese, Parmesan cheese and milk until smooth and creamy. In a deep saucepan, in a large amount of rapidly boiling water, cook fettucine until tender (dry 8–10 minutes, fresh 3–5 minutes); stir occasionally to separate. Drain well; combine with margarine and cheese mixture. Toss until completely coated. Season with pepper. Serve immediately.

Makes 4 servings.

Calories per serving: 329   Thiamin: Excellent   Vitamin A: Good

PRIMAVERA PASTA

Preparation: 10 minutes   Cook: 5–8 minutes

It's possible to make a gourmet dinner in minutes with a recipe like Primavera Pasta served with grilled salmon in Seafood Marinade (page 77) and a green salad. Use either fresh or dried commercial pasta, such as fusilli, fettucine or linguine. If fresh pasta is available in your market, it cooks in half the time.

½ cup	Becel Margarine, divided	125 mL
½ cup	sliced fresh mushrooms	125 mL
1	medium onion, chopped	1
½	EACH: medium green pepper and medium red pepper, chopped	½
1 tsp	EACH: tarragon, basil	5 mL
½ lb	fresh *or* dried pasta	250 g
¼ cup	Black Diamond Grated Parmesan Cheese	50 mL
¼ tsp	freshly ground black pepper	1 mL
1 tbsp	chopped fresh parsley	15 mL

In a small saucepan, over medium-high heat, melt ¼ cup (50 mL) margarine. Sauté mushrooms, onion and peppers with seasonings until tender-crisp, about 5 minutes; keep warm. Meanwhile, cook pasta in rapidly boiling water, (fresh 3–5 minutes, dry 8–10 minutes); drain well. Toss with vegetable mixture, remaining margarine, cheese and pepper. Sprinkle with parsley and serve.

Makes 4 servings.

Calories per serving: 492   Vitamins A and C; thiamin: Excellent   Iron: Good

PESTO PASTA

Preparation: about 10 minutes   Cook: 3–8 minutes

This is the most authentic use of Pesto Sauce, which is a specialty of Italy.

1 lb	narrow noodles (e.g. fettucine, linguine)	500 g
¼ cup	heavy cream	50 mL
1 cup	Hurry-Up Pesto Sauce (page 12)	250 mL
¼ tsp	freshly ground black pepper	1 mL
¼ cup	Black Diamond Grated Parmesan Cheese	50 mL

In a deep saucepan, in a large amount of rapidly boiling water, cook pasta until tender (dry 8–10 minutes; fresh 3–5 minutes); stir occasionally to separate. Drain well; return to saucepan and combine with cream, Pesto Sauce, pepper and cheese. Stir and heat through. Serve immediately.

Makes 4–6 servings.

TIP: Add a spoonful of margarine to the water when cooking pasta to prevent boil-overs.

Calories per serving: 447   Vitamins A and thiamin: Excellent   Calcium, iron and vitamin C: Good

APPLE RICE PILAF

Preparation: 10 minutes   Cook: about 20 minutes

In a pilaf, rice is browned in oil or margarine to coat the kernels and to keep them separated during cooking. While chicken broth is generally used, our method uses apple juice. Try it for a Sunday family dinner with a roast of pork and peas mixed with mushrooms.

1 cup	uncooked long-grain white rice	250 mL
2 tbsp	Becel Margarine, melted	25 mL
2 cups	apple juice	500 mL
1	red apple, cored and chopped	1
¼ cup	chopped dry roasted peanuts	50 mL
1 tbsp	chopped fresh parsley	15 mL

Microwave: In an 8-cup (2 L) covered casserole, melt margarine at HIGH (100%) 30 seconds. Stir in rice, heat at HIGH 2–3 minutes; stir once. Add liquid and heat, covered, at MEDIUM-HIGH (70%) 13–16 minutes. Add chopped apple and peanuts, and heat, covered, at MEDIUM-HIGH 1–2 minutes. Let stand, covered, 5–10 minutes. Sprinkle with parsley and serve.

Makes 4 servings.

In a large skillet, sauté rice in margarine until golden brown, about 5 minutes. Add apple juice, bring to a boil, then reduce heat, cover and simmer 15–20 minutes. Add apple and peanuts during the last 5 minutes. Sprinkle with parsley and serve.

TIPS: 1. For softer rice, increase liquid and cook longer; for firmer rice, decrease liquid and cook for a shorter time. 2. Unsweetened canned pineapple tidbits and juice may replace apple and apple juice. 3. For a milder flavor, use 1 cup (250 mL) apple juice and 1 cup (250 mL) water.

Calories per serving: 286   Vitamin C: Excellent   Fiber: Good

Clockwise: Apricot-Stuffed Lamb Chops (page 62); Mixed Seafood Brochette (page 78); Stir-Fry Pork Tenderloin and Vegetables on a bed of rice (page 59)

TUNA RICE SALAD

Preparation: about 20 minutes   Chill: 30 minutes

Tuna is one staple that's usually in everyone's kitchen. Lift it out of the ordinary by combining it with nutty and nutritious brown rice.

1 tbsp	Yolk-Free Mayonnaise (page 38)	15 mL
1 tsp	curry powder	5 mL
2 cups	cooked brown rice	500 mL
1	can (7½ oz/213 g) tuna packed in water, drained	1
½	red pepper, finely chopped	½
½	green apple, cored and diced	½
1 tbsp	chopped chives	15 mL
¼ cup	chopped raisins	50 mL
¼ tsp	ground nutmeg	1 mL

In a small bowl, combine mayonnaise and curry powder. In a salad bowl, mix remaining ingredients except nutmeg; add dressing and toss well. Sprinkle with nutmeg. Chill 30 minutes before serving.

Makes 4 main course servings.

TIP: For 2 cups (500 mL) cooked brown rice, you'll require about 3/4 cup (175 mL) uncooked brown rice to 1½ cups (375 mL) water; cook for approximately 45 minutes.

Calories per serving: 224   Vitamin C: Good

LIPTON ONION 'N HERBS RICE MIX

Preparation: about 5 minutes

Herbs and Lipton Soup Mix give a quick change of taste to the blandness of rice. This is a convenient addition for your shortcut shelf.

1 pouch	Lipton Onion or Onion-Mushroom Soup	1
2 cups	uncooked long-grain white rice	500 mL
2 tbsp	parsley flakes	25 mL
1½ tsp	basil	7 mL

Combine all ingredients; store in a covered container.

Makes 2½ cups (625 mL) rice mix.

ONION 'N HERBS RICE   Preparation: about 5 minutes   Cook: about 20 minutes

2 cups	water	500 mL
1 tbsp	margarine or butter	15 mL
1¼ cups	Lipton Onion 'n Herbs Rice Mix	300 mL

In a medium saucepan, bring water to a boil. Add margarine. Stir rice mix thoroughly be-

fore adding to water. Simmer, covered, 15–20 minutes or until rice is tender.

Microwave: In an 8-cup (2 L) covered casserole, bring water and margarine to a boil at HIGH (100%). Stir in rice mix; heat, covered, at MEDIUM-HIGH (70%) 13–16 minutes. Let stand, covered, 5–10 minutes.

Makes approximately 6 servings.

Calories per serving: 93

VARIATIONS

Slivered toasted almonds, raisins or cut-up fruit may be added.

TIPS: Margarine or butter is added to help keep rice separated. For fluffy rice, allow to stand 5 minutes. Fluff with fork before serving.

Clockwise: Mexican Coffee (page 148); Ice Cream Tacos (page 139); Chicken Mole (page 73); Ensalada de Noche Buena (page 32)

FIESTA RICE

Preparation: about 10 minutes   Cook: about 30 minutes

This recipe gives a gourmet's touch to Mexican Rice. Mildly flavored and mildly seasoned, it is a pleasant accompaniment to spicy tacos.

1 cup	uncooked long-grain white rice	250 mL
2 tbsp	vegetable oil	25 mL
1¾ cups	water	425 mL
1	package MexiCasa Mexican Rice Seasoning Mix	1
½ cup	grated Black Diamond Medium Cheddar Cheese	125 mL
2 tbsp	chopped green pepper	25 mL
1 tbsp	chopped pimiento	15 mL
2 tbsp	sliced black olives (optional)	25 mL

In a large skillet, sauté rice in hot oil until golden brown, about 5 minutes. Add water and seasoning mix; blend thoroughly. Bring to a boil, then reduce heat, cover and simmer 20 minutes. Gently stir in remaining ingredients; cover and heat thoroughly 3–5 minutes.

Microwave: In an 8-cup (2 L) covered casserole, combine rice and oil. Heat at HIGH (100%) 2–3 minutes; stir once. Add water and seasoning mix, heat, covered, at MEDIUM-HIGH (70%) 13–16 minutes. Add remaining ingredients. Let stand, covered, 5–10 minutes.

Makes approximately 4 servings.

Calories per serving: 151   Vitamin C: Excellent   Fiber: Good

CHEATER'S SPECIAL POTATOES

Preparation: about 10 minutes   Cook: about 35 minutes

When I was first served these potatoes, I found it hard to believe my friend had used "cheater's shortcuts." Now it's one of my favorite fast recipes.

3 tbsp	melted margarine *or* butter, divided	45 mL
1	envelope Lipton Cream of Chicken Cup-a-Soup	1
⅔ cup	dairy sour cream *or* yogurt	150 mL
2 tsp	minced onion	10 mL
2 cups	frozen hash brown potatoes	500 mL
1 cup	slivered almonds	250 mL
	Bacon bits (optional)	

In a 6-cup (1.5 L) casserole, place 2 tbsp (25 mL) melted margarine. Prepare soup mix according to package directions. Stir soup, sour cream, onion and potatoes into casserole. Toss almonds with remaining margarine; sprinkle over pota-toes. Add bacon bits if desired. Bake at 350°F (180°C) 35–45 minutes.

Microwave: In a 6-cup (1.5 L) casserole, melt margarine at HIGH (100%) 45 seconds. Remove 1 tbsp (15 mL); set aside. Prepare soup mix according to package directions. Stir soup, sour cream, onion and potatoes into casserole. Toss almonds in remaining margarine (add paprika for deeper color, if desired); sprinkle over potatoes. Cover with waxed paper. Heat at MEDIUM-HIGH (70%) 12–15 minutes; rotate casserole once. Let stand 5 minutes.

Makes 4–6 servings.

TIP: Substitute ⅔ cup (150 mL) Classic Lipton Onion Dip (page 10) for sour cream and onions.

Calories per serving: 407   Iron and vitamin C: Good

POTATO AND MUSHROOM MEDLEY

Preparation: about 10 minutes   Cook: 10 minutes

When you're cooking potatoes, double the amount required and you'll have a head start on this recipe.

1	small onion, finely chopped	1
2 tbsp	Becel Margarine, melted	25 mL
2 cups	diced, cooked potatoes	500 mL
1 cup	sliced mushrooms	250 mL
⅛ tsp	EACH: salt, pepper	0.5 mL
1 cup	grated, low-fat cheese	250 mL

In a medium skillet, sauté onion in margarine until tender. Add potatoes and mushrooms and cook approximately 5 minutes. Add seasonings and sprinkle cheese over top. Reduce heat, cover and cook until cheese melts, about 5 minutes.

Makes 4 servings.

TIP: For a new taste, cook potatoes in beef or chicken broth.

Calories per serving: 218   Calcium: Excellent

ENCORE POTATOES

Preparation: about 30 minutes   Chill: 2–3 hours or overnight   Cook: 40 minutes

This recipe title says it all — everyone always asks for seconds. To use this outstanding dish for a party, make it the night before to simplify last-minute preparations.

6	large potatoes, peeled and halved	6
1	container (500 mL) dairy sour cream	1
1½ cups	grated Black Diamond Old Cheddar Cheese, divided	375 mL
6	green onions, chopped	6
1½ tsp	salt	7 mL
¼ tsp	EACH: pepper, paprika	1 mL

In a large saucepan, cook potatoes until fork-tender; drain. Into a large bowl, grate potatoes; stir in sour cream, 1 cup (250 mL) cheese, onions, salt and pepper. Turn into a greased 8-cup (2 L) casserole. Sprinkle with paprika. Cover and chill 2–3 hours or overnight. Bake, uncovered, at 350°F (180°C) 30–40 minutes or until heated through. Sprinkle with remaining cheese during last 10 minutes.

Microwave: Assemble casserole as above. Cover with waxed paper. Heat at MEDIUM-HIGH (70%) 12–15 minutes; rotate casserole once. Sprinkle with remaining cheese. Let stand 5 minutes.

Makes 6–8 servings.

TIP: A 1 kg package of frozen hash browns may be used instead of cooked potatoes.

Calories per serving: 283   Vitamin A: Excellent   Calcium and vitamin C: Good

LITE AND CREAMY POTATOES

Preparation: about 5 minutes   Cook: about 20 minutes

Dill has a particular affinity for new potatoes and yogurt. This low-calorie dish is even more attractive with small, red new potatoes.

6	small new potatoes	6
½ cup	plain yogurt *or* dairy sour cream	125 mL
½ tsp	Lawry's Seasoned Salt	2 mL
1 tsp	dill weed	5 mL

Scrub potatoes and pierce skin. In a saucepan, cook potatoes covered in a small amount of boiling water 20–25 minutes or until potatoes are tender; drain. Combine remaining ingredients; stir into potatoes.

Makes 3–4 servings.

TIP: Add powdered milk to overcooked mashed potatoes for a fluffier texture.

Calories per serving: 151   Vitamin C: Excellent   Fiber: Good   Low fat

GRILLED LEMON POTATOES

Preparation: about 5 minutes   Cook: 45 minutes

Lemon enhances the flavor of potatoes. These are the best grilled potatoes I have ever tasted.

3	large baking potatoes	3
½ cup	margarine *or* butter	125 mL
½ tsp	Lawry's Garlic Salt with Parsley	2 mL
1 tbsp	lemon juice	15 mL
1 tbsp	Lawry's Seasoned Salt	15 mL
1¼ tsp	Lawry's Lemon Pepper	6 mL

Cut potatoes in half lengthwise; deeply score cut surfaces. Cover skin side with aluminum foil. In a small skillet, melt margarine; add remaining ingredients. Generously brush cut side of potatoes with sauce. Place potatoes, foil side down, on grill. Cook until tender, about 45 minutes. Turn cut side down occasionally during cooking.

Makes 6 servings.

TIP: Thread small or cubed par-boiled potatoes with fish and vegetables on skewers. Brush with Lemon Sauce (above recipe).

Calories per serving: 254   Vitamins A and C: Good

CRISP ONION-ROASTED POTATOES

Preparation: under 10 minutes   Cook: 60 minutes

This is one of my favorite potato recipes for serving with beef — either a roast or steaks from the barbecue.

1	pouch Lipton Onion *or* Onion-Mushroom Soup	1
½ cup	olive *or* vegetable oil	125 mL
¼ cup	margarine *or* butter, melted	50 mL
1 tsp	EACH: thyme leaves, marjoram leaves (optional)	5 mL
¼ tsp	pepper	1 mL
2 lb	all-purpose potatoes, washed and cut into quarters	1 kg
	Fresh chopped parsley (optional)	

In a shallow baking pan, blend all ingredients except potatoes. Add potatoes and turn to coat thoroughly. Bake at 450°F (230°C) 60 minutes or until potatoes are tender and golden brown; stir potatoes occasionally. Garnish, if desired, with parsley.

Makes approximately 8 servings.

Calories per serving: 320   Vitamin C: Excellent

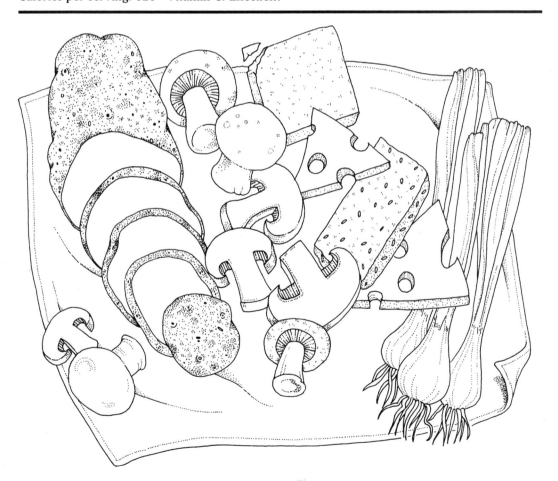

VEGETABLES

A few years ago when I was teaching adult cooking classes, attendance fell off for the vegetable class if I announced it ahead of time. When I started calling it "The Forgotten Guest," attendance returned to normal. Needless to say, in this section, vegetables are "The Guests of Honor." For those classes I also devised the "rule of least" for cooking vegetables — least peeling, least waiting before cooking, least water, least time to cook, least heat to keep water boiling, least waiting after cooking. Today vegetable consumption has increased because there is more awareness and interest in health needs. Quickly prepared vegetables can be stir-fried, sautéed, steamed or microwaved in minutes. Vegetables are very successful in the microwave because of their high moisture content. They remain fresh-tasting and are extra-nutritious. The cooking time can be made even shorter by cutting the vegetables into bite-size pieces. Remember they are at their best when they are cooked to tender-crisp.

QUICK SEASONING TIPS

In order to ensure a year-round supply of your favorite fresh herbs, grow an herb garden at your kitchen doorstep in the summer and on your window sill in the winter. Then experiment to find the herb and vegetable combinations you prefer. Until you become familiar with the taste of individual herbs, you might like to make up a mixture that blends well with vegetables. Mix together 1 tbsp (15 mL) each: parsley, chives, chervil and thyme. Sprinkle some on your vegetables, along with salt and pepper. Or, add some of the herb mixture to melted margarine or butter to make a sauce. Of course lemon juice is always a perfect seasoning for green vegetables.

CREATIVE GARNISHING TIPS

Because vegetables are so attractive and colorful, they need only simple garnishes. Glazing vegetables highlights the color and enhances it. Beets especially benefit from a sweet-sour glazing with an orange twist garnish. Plain cooked vegetables like sliced carrots only need a sprinkling of chopped parsley, watercress, mint or dill for contrast. Try a drift of sliced mushrooms and bacon bits on a serving bowl of peas. Creamed vegetables are even more attractive with a topping of grated cheese, snippets of herbs or pimiento. A classic way to serve asparagus is with chopped hard-cooked egg. Give it pizazz by making a multi-color garnish of chopped cooked egg white, chopped pimiento and chopped black olive.

ASPARAGUS WITH ORANGE SAUCE

Preparation: about 10 minutes   Cook: 10 minutes

If fresh asparagus is unavailable, this pungent-sweet recipe will help to perk up frozen asparagus.

2 lb	asparagus, trimmed	1 kg
½ cup	Becel Margarine, divided	125 mL
⅓ cup	sliced green onions	75 mL
1 tsp	Dijon mustard	5 mL
1⅓ cups	orange juice	325 mL
6	orange wedges	6

In a large skillet, add asparagus to 1 inch (2.5 cm) boiling water; simmer, uncovered, until barely tender when pierced, 3–5 minutes; drain. Keep warm. In a saucepan, over medium heat, melt 1 tbsp (15 mL) margarine. Add green onions and stir until limp. Add mustard and orange juice. Boil, uncovered, over high heat until reduced to ⅔ cup (150 mL). Reduce heat to low and add remaining margarine. Lay asparagus on warmed plates and pour orange sauce over it. Garnish with orange wedges.

Microwave: Cook asparagus in 2 tbsp (25 mL) water, covered, at HIGH (100%) 4–5 minutes until tender-crisp; drain. In a 2-cup (500 mL) measure, heat margarine and green onions at HIGH 1–2 minutes. Add mustard and orange juice. Heat at HIGH 5–7 minutes. Pour over asparagus and serve.

Makes 6 servings.

Calories per serving: 228   Vitamins A and C: Excellent   Fiber: Good

BROCCOLI CASSEROLE

Preparation: about 10 minutes   Cook: about 30 minutes

Creamed broccoli is given an extra tang when yogurt is used in the sauce.

2	packages (300 g) frozen chopped broccoli, partially thawed	2
⅓ cup	Becel Margarine, divided	75 mL
3 tbsp	all-purpose flour	45 mL
⅛ tsp	pepper	0.5 mL
1½ cups	skim milk	375 mL
1	OXO Chicken Bouillon Cube, crushed	1
¼ cup	grated carrot	50 mL
¼–½ cup	finely diced onion	50–125 mL
½ cup	skim milk yogurt	125 mL
1 cup	seasoned croutons	250 mL

Place broccoli in a lightly greased casserole dish. In a saucepan, melt margarine over medium heat. Remove 3 tbsp (45 mL) and set aside. Blend in flour and pepper. Gradually add milk and continue cooking, stirring until mixture thickens, about 5 minutes. Remove from heat. Add bouillon cube, carrot, onion and yogurt. Pour over broccoli. Mix croutons with reserved margarine and sprinkle over casserole. Bake at 350°F (180°C) 30–35 minutes or until hot.

Microwave: In an 8-cup (2 L) casserole, melt margarine at HIGH (100%) 45–60 seconds. Remove 3 tbsp (45 mL) and set aside. Stir in flour and pepper. Gradually stir in milk. Heat at HIGH 5–7 minutes, stirring every 2 minutes until thickened. Stir in bouillon cube, carrot, onion and yogurt. Add broccoli. Mix croutons with reserved margarine; sprinkle over broccoli. Add paprika, if desired. Cover with waxed paper. Heat at HIGH 8–10 minutes or until heated through. Rotate dish once. Let stand, covered, 5 minutes.

Makes 6 servings.

Calories per serving: 187   Fiber; vitamins A and C: Good   Calcium: Good

ISLAND BAKED BEANS

Preparation: about 5 minutes   Standing: 1 hour   Cook: 1½ hours

No one will guess you used a shortcut and made this recipe with canned beans. The rum adds a special flavor. If you prefer, you can use pineapple juice for another tropical variation.

2	cans (14 oz/398 mL) baked beans	2
1	can (19 oz/540 mL) sliced pineapple, drained (reserve juice)	1
½ cup	brown sugar, firmly packed	125 mL
⅓ cup	rum *or* reserved pineapple juice	75 mL
¼ cup	finely chopped onion	50 mL
1 tbsp	instant coffee granules	15 mL
1 tsp	dry mustard	5 mL
6	slices bacon	6

In an 11 × 7-inch (2 L) baking dish, combine beans, ¼ cup (50 mL) pineapple juice, brown sugar, rum, onion, instant coffee and mustard. Let stand at room temperature 1 hour. Arrange bacon slices on top of beans and pineapple slices on top of bacon. Bake, uncovered, at 375°F (190°C) 1½ hours.

Microwave: Assemble casserole as above. Heat, covered, at HIGH (100%) 10–15 minutes; stir once.

Makes 8–10 servings.

Calories per serving: 210   Vitamin C: Good

ZESTY ITALIAN PASTA-BEAN BAKE

Preparation: about 10 minutes   Cook: 30 minutes

Meatless entrées are a great help in cutting food costs—an important consideration with today's high cost of living.

¼ cup	Becel Margarine, divided	50 mL
1	large onion, sliced	1
1	clove garlic, minced	1
½	medium green pepper, chopped	½
1 cup	sliced mushrooms	250 mL
1	can (19 oz/540 mL) red kidney beans, undrained	1
1½ cups	shell or elbow macaroni, cooked	375 mL
1	can (14 oz/398 mL) tomato sauce	1
¼ tsp	EACH: oregano, pepper	1 mL
½ tsp	salt	2 mL
½ cup	coarse bread crumbs	125 mL
2 tbsp	Black Diamond Grated Parmesan Cheese	25 mL

In a medium skillet, melt 2 tbsp (25 mL) margarine; sauté onion, garlic, green pepper and mushrooms. Stir in kidney beans, pasta, tomato sauce, oregano, pepper and salt. Place in a greased 6-cup (1.5 L) casserole dish. In a small bowl, toss bread crumbs and cheese with remaining melted margarine. Sprinkle over casserole. Bake, uncovered, at 350°F (180°C) 20 minutes.

Microwave: In a 6-cup (1.5 L) casserole, melt margarine at HIGH (100%) 45 seconds; reserve 2 tbsp (25 mL). Add onion, garlic, green pepper and mushrooms. Heat at HIGH 3–4 minutes. Complete as above. Heat at HIGH 8–10 minutes. Let stand, covered, 5 minutes.

Makes 4–6 servings.

Calories per serving: 245   Fiber and vitamin C: Excellent   Iron and vitamin A: Good

SPICY REFRIED BEANS

Preparation: about 5 minutes   Cook: 25 minutes

Because of my interest in Mexican food, I attended several cooking schools in Mexico. Much to my surprise, I discovered traditional Mexican meals including breakfast are accompanied by refried beans!

2	cans MexiCasa Refried Beans	2
1	package MexiCasa Taco Seasoning Mix	1
2 cups	grated Black Diamond Cheddar Cheese	500 mL
2 tbsp	finely chopped onion	25 mL

In a medium casserole, combine all ingredients. Cover and bake at 325°F (160°C) 25 minutes.

Microwave: Assemble casserole as above. Heat, covered, on HIGH (100%) 7–8 minutes; stir once.

Makes approximately 4 cups (1 L).

TIP: Assemble this quick and easy dish ahead and bake just before serving.

Calories per ½ cup (125 mL) serving: 409   Calcium: Excellent   Vitamin A: Good

SCALLOPED CORN

Preparation: about 10 minutes   Cook: about 30 minutes

I still remember the welcoming warmth of the scalloped corn dish my mother made for winter dinners. While the old-fashioned goodness has been retained in this recipe, it has been updated for modern health concerns.

¼ cup	Becel Margarine, divided	50 mL
2 tbsp	all-purpose flour	25 mL
½ tsp	dry mustard	2 mL
¼ tsp	ground nutmeg	1 mL
⅛ tsp	EACH: salt, pepper	0.5 mL
1¼ cups	skim milk	300 mL
1	package (300 g) frozen corn kernels, thawed and drained	1
1	medium egg, lightly beaten	1
½ cup	coarsely crumbled unsalted soda crackers	125 mL
	Paprika	

In a large saucepan, melt margarine; remove 2 tbsp (25 mL) and set aside. Stir in flour, mustard, nutmeg, salt and pepper; cook 1 minute. Stir in milk. Cook until smooth and thickened.

Stir in corn and egg. Pour into a greased 4-cup (1 L) casserole; sprinkle with cracker crumbs and paprika. Drizzle remaining margarine over crackers. Bake at 350°F (180°C) 30–35 minutes or until lightly browned.

Microwave: In a 6-cup (1.5 L) casserole, melt margarine at HIGH (100%) 45–60 seconds. Remove 2 tbsp (25 mL) and set aside. Stir in flour, mustard, nutmeg, salt and pepper. Gradually stir in milk. Heat at HIGH 5–7 minutes; stir every 2 minutes, until thickened. Stir in corn and egg. Sprinkle with cracker crumbs and paprika; drizzle with reserved margarine and cover with waxed paper. Heat at MEDIUM-HIGH (70%) 12–14 minutes; rotate once or twice during cooking. Let stand, covered, 5 minutes.

Makes 6 servings.

Calories per serving: 169

CARIBBEAN CARROTS

Preparation: about 10 minutes   Cook: about 15 minutes

Coconut adds a tropical touch to these gingered carrots.

2 cups	carrots, peeled and thinly sliced	500 g
2 tbsp	Becel Margarine, melted	25 mL
¾ tsp	finely chopped candied ginger	3 mL
	Lawry's Garlic Salt with Parsley, to taste	
2–3 tbsp	shredded coconut, toasted	25–45 mL

Cook carrots until tender; drain. Add margarine, ginger and garlic salt; mix well. Sprinkle coconut over carrots.

Microwave: Cook carrots in 2 tbsp (25 mL) water, covered, at HIGH (100%) 8–10 minutes until tender-crisp; drain. Add margarine, ginger and garlic salt; mix well. Sprinkle coconut over carrots.

Makes 4 servings.

TIP: To chop candied ginger, use kitchen scissors and snip; dip scissors in hot water frequently for easier cutting.

Calories per serving: 121   Vitamin A: Excellent   Iron and fiber: Good

ROASTED CORN ON THE COB

Preparation: about 5 minutes   Cook: 20 minutes

For the most delectable corn you'll ever taste, try a novel cooking method—barbecue it wrapped in its own husks. Be sure to use corn that's been picked the same day as it has the best flavor. Set out lots of seasoned margarine and enjoy a healthy heart treat!

8	ears corn (with husks)	8
½ cup	Becel Margarine	125 mL
1 tbsp	Lawry's Seasoned Salt	15 mL
1 tsp	Lawry's Seasoned Pepper	5 mL

Peel husks back carefully and remove silk. Combine margarine, seasoned salt and seasoned pepper; spread over each ear. Smooth husks over corn and tie ends together with string. Arrange corn over medium-hot coals. Roast about 20 minutes, turning every 5 minutes.

Microwave: Prepare corn as above except do not tie with string. Arrange 4 cobs of corn in oven with some space between each one. Microwave at HIGH (100%) 12–17 minutes, in husks (less if husks removed). Rearrange cobs once during cooking. Let stand 5 minutes. Repeat with remaining cobs.

Makes 8 ears.

TIPS: The corn can be husked, seasoned, wrapped in aluminum foil and roasted the same way on the barbecue; or wrap in waxed paper for microwave cooking. However, leaving the husks on gives a more intense flavor and a feeling of freshness. Gloves or paper napkins are needed in order to husk the corn once roasted.

Calories per ear: 185   Fiber and vitamin A: Good

CUCUMBER AND SEAFOOD BOATS

Preparation: about 10 minutes   Cook: 15 minutes

Pack a hamper with these Cucumber and Seafood Boats, a salad, fruit and chilled wine for an unforgettable picnic.

3	medium, firm cucumbers	3
1½ cups	cooked seafood (e.g., tuna, salmon, shrimp, leftover cooked fillets)	375 mL
3	green onions, finely chopped	3
1 tsp	soy sauce	5 mL
1	egg, beaten	1
	Black Diamond Grated Parmesan Cheese	

Peel cucumbers and cut lengthwise; scoop out seeds. In a mixing bowl, combine seafood, green onions, soy sauce and egg. Stuff cucumbers with this mixture. Sprinkle with cheese and bake on a greased baking sheet at 350°F (180°C) about 15 minutes. Serve warm or cold.

Microwave: Heat prepared cucumbers at HIGH (100%) 5–7 minutes.

Makes 6 servings.

Calories per serving: 135   Vitamins A and C: Good

CAPONATA

Preparation: about 15 minutes   Cook: 25 minutes

This Sicilian recipe can be served hot as a vegetable dish for supper or as an hors d'oeuvre. Served cold, it is a delicious accompaniment for sliced meats or a hearty topping for thick slices of Italian bread.

1	medium eggplant, peeled and diced	1
½ cup	Becel Margarine, divided	125 mL
1	clove garlic, minced	1
1	medium onion, chopped	1
½ cup	EACH: chopped celery, green pepper, tomato sauce	125 mL
2 tbsp	vinegar	25 mL
1 tbsp	EACH: sugar, capers	15 mL
1 tbsp	EACH: anchovies, olives (optional)	15 mL

In a large skillet, over high heat, sauté eggplant in ¼ cup (50 mL) margarine for 5 minutes; set aside. Melt remaining margarine and sauté garlic, onion, celery and green pepper until softened; add tomato sauce. Cover, simmer slowly, about 5 minutes. Add vinegar, sugar, capers, and eggplant. Simmer, uncovered, 15 minutes, or until thickened; stir occasionally. Chill, add anchovies and olives if desired before serving.

Microwave: In an 8-cup (2 L) covered casserole, melt margarine at HIGH (100%) 1½ minutes. Stir in garlic, onion, celery and green pepper. Heat, covered, at HIGH 2 minutes. Stir in eggplant; cook, covered, at HIGH 3–5 minutes; stir once. Add tomato sauce, vinegar, sugar and capers. Heat, uncovered, at HIGH 8–10 minutes until slightly thickened and vegetables are soft; stir occasionally. Complete as above.

Makes approximately 4 main course or 8 appetizer servings.

TIP: Caponata will keep in the refrigerator for one week.

Calories per main course serving: 257   Vitamins A and C: Excellent

PIQUANT CAULIFLOWER

Preparation: about 5 minutes   Cook: about 10 minutes

This recipe gives some zing to cauliflower or Brussels sprouts.

1	medium head cauliflower, trimmed	1
	or	
4 cups	Brussels sprouts	1 L
1/3 cup	margarine *or* butter, melted	75 mL
1 tbsp	prepared mustard	15 mL
1 tsp	Worcestershire sauce	5 mL
1/2 tsp	Lawry's Seasoned Salt	2 mL
Dash	Lawry's Seasoned Pepper	Dash

Break cauliflower into florets; cook and drain. Combine remaining ingredients, pour over cauliflower and heat.

Microwave: Cook cauliflower in 1/4 cup (50 mL) water, covered, at HIGH (100%) 6–8 minutes until tender-crisp; drain. Combine remaining ingredients, pour over cauliflower and heat at HIGH 1–2 minutes.

Makes 4 servings.

Calories per serving: 136   Vitamins A and C: Good

BATTER-FRIED ONION RINGS

Preparation: 10 minutes   Cook: about 10 minutes

Using pancake mix for batter makes short work of fried onion rings.

1 lb	large onions	500 g
1 cup	pancake mix	250 mL
1	egg	1
1 tbsp	vegetable oil	15 mL
1	OXO Chicken Bouillon Cube	1
1/2 cup	boiling water	125 mL
	Oil for frying	

Cut onions in medium slices. Break into rings. In a small bowl, combine pancake mix with egg and oil. Dissolve bouillon cube in boiling water; stir into batter. Dip onion rings, one by one, into the batter; drain off excess batter. In a large skillet, over medium-high heat, heat 1 inch (2.5 cm) oil. Fry onion rings in oil until golden brown, about 4 minutes; turn once during cooking. Keep warm until ready to serve.

Makes 6 servings.

TIP: Taste while you cook! When using OXO Cubes with liquids that may contain salt, or, when adding OXO Cubes to perk up the flavor of favorite recipes, taste before you add salt.

Calories per serving: approximately 224

MINTED HERB PEAS

Preparation: under 5 minutes   Cook: about 5 minutes

If you're tired of serving peas in the same old way, try this herb combination. I sometimes prefer the French method of cooking them by using torn lettuce leaves in the bottom of the saucepan. This eliminates the need for water.

2 cups	frozen peas	500 mL
2 tbsp	Becel Margarine, melted	25 mL
1 tsp	dried mint, crushed	5 mL
1/4 tsp	EACH: basil, oregano	1 mL

Cook peas according to package directions; drain. Add margarine and seasonings; mix well.

Makes 3–4 servings.

Calories per serving: 102   Fiber: Good   Vitamins A and C: Good

CREAMED SPINACH

Preparation: about 5 minutes   Cook: 15 minutes

Guests request this recipe so many times at Lawry's The Prime Rib Restaurant that cards have been printed for them. It is traditionally served with prime ribs of beef, Yorkshire pudding and baked potatoes. Now you can try this tempting dish at home.

1	package (300 g) frozen chopped spinach	1
	or	
1	bunch spinach, chopped and cooked	1
2	bacon slices, finely chopped	2
1/2 cup	finely chopped onion	125 mL
2 tbsp	all-purpose flour	25 mL
1 tsp	Lawry's Seasoned Salt	5 mL
1/4 tsp	Lawry's Seasoned Pepper	1 mL
1	clove garlic, minced	1
1 cup	milk	250 mL

Cook spinach according to package directions; drain well. Meanwhile, in a small skillet, sauté bacon and onions, about 10 minutes. Remove from heat. Add flour, seasoned salt, seasoned pepper and garlic. Blend thoroughly. Slowly add milk, return to heat and stir until thickened. Add spinach, mix thoroughly and serve.

Microwave: Heat spinach at HIGH (100%) 3–4 minutes; drain. In a small casserole, heat bacon and onions at HIGH 3–4 minutes. Stir in flour and seasonings. Slowly add milk; heat 2–3 minutes at HIGH until thickened, stirring twice. Add spinach; mix well.

Makes 4 servings.

TIPS: When using garlic, remove outer skin and place in a garlic press. Crush and scrape off the garlic that comes through the press with a knife. Repeat one or two more times to get as much from the clove as possible. If you don't have a garlic press, mince very fine.

Calories per serving: 92   Vitamin A: Excellent   Calcium and vitamin C: Good

DIETER'S SPINACH QUICHE

Preparation: under 10 minutes   Cook: 35 minutes

Whenever you are counting calories, whip up this vegetable dish to serve at brunch or supper. It's also a great appetizer for a party.

1/2 cup	Country Crock Margarine, melted	125 mL
1 cup	all-purpose flour	250 mL
3/4 tsp	Blue Ribbon Double Action Baking Powder	3 mL
2	eggs	2
3/4 cup	skim milk	175 mL
1/2 lb	grated Black Diamond Mozzarella Cheese	250 g
1	package (10 oz) fresh spinach, chopped	1

In a large bowl, blend margarine, flour, baking powder, eggs and milk. Stir in cheese and spinach. Pour into 2 greased 9-inch (23 cm) pie plates. Bake at 375°F (190°C) 30–35 minutes. Let stand 10 minutes and cut in sections. Serve warm or chill.

Microwave: Combine all ingredients as above. Heat at MEDIUM-HIGH (70%) 6–8 minutes or until almost set in the center. Rotate the dish part way through. Let stand 10 minutes.

Makes 8 servings.

Calories per serving: 257   Vitamin A: Excellent   Calcium and vitamin C: Good

HARVEST SQUASH

Preparation: about 10 minutes   Cook: 1 hour

Butternut or pepper squash can be steamed in advance and refrigerated until you're ready to complete this recipe. Then bake it along with a leg of lamb. Serve it with Minted Herb Peas (page 103) and warm rolls for an easy oven meal.

2	medium squash (e.g. pepper, acorn, butternut)	2
2 tbsp	margarine *or* butter, melted	25 mL
1 tsp	Lawry's Seasoned Salt	5 mL
1/4 cup	EACH: diced onion, celery	50 mL
1/2 cup	grated Black Diamond Cheddar *or* Parmesan Cheese	125 mL
1/8 tsp	Lawry's Seasoned Pepper	0.5 mL

Cut squash in half; remove seeds and pierce centers. Arrange, cut side up, in an oblong baking dish. Combine margarine, seasoned salt, onion and celery; spoon into squash cavities. Cover and bake at 350°F (180°C) about 1 hour or until tender. Uncover during last 10 minutes; top with cheese and continue baking until cheese melts and squash is tender. Sprinkle with seasoned pepper.

Microwave: Pierce skin of whole squash several times; place on a platter on paper towels. Heat at HIGH (100%) 4–5 minutes; turn squash once. Let stand 3 minutes. (This makes it easier to cut squash in half.) Cut squash in half; remove seeds and pierce centers. Arrange, cut side up, in an oblong baking dish. Combine margarine, seasonings, onion and celery; spoon into squash cavities. Heat, covered with plastic wrap, at HIGH 4–6 minutes or until squash is tender. Sprinkle with cheese; let stand, covered, 2 minutes.

Makes 6–8 servings.

Calories per serving: 92   Vitamin A: Excellent   Vitamin C: Good

HERBED TOMATOES

Preparation: about 5 minutes   Cook: 15 minutes

Baked tomatoes are an attractive and colorful side dish, which should be served more often. To keep them round and plump, since they tend to lose their shape while baking, place them in lightly greased custard cups before you pop them into the oven.

4	medium tomatoes	4
1 tbsp	lemon juice	15 mL
	Lawry's Seasoned Salt and Seasoned Pepper	
1 tbsp	Becel Margarine	15 mL
2 tsp	chopped fresh parsley	10 mL
1 tsp	EACH: chopped chives, basil	5 mL

Slice top off each tomato; put tomatoes into a greased shallow dish or custard cups. Sprinkle lemon juice, seasoned salt and seasoned pepper over cut top of tomatoes. Bake at 350°F (180°C) 10 minutes. Remove from oven, dot each tomato with margarine; sprinkle with parsley, chives and basil; bake for 5 minutes longer.

Microwave: Prepare tomatoes as above. Heat, covered, at HIGH (100%) 5–7 minutes.

Makes 4 servings.

Calories per serving: 50   Vitamins A and C: Excellent

FESTIVE BRANDIED YAMS

Preparation: about 15 minutes   Cook: about 30 minutes

These sweetly glazed yams are ideal for holiday entertaining. They are plentiful in the fall and winter and complement turkey, Rock Cornish hens and ham.

1	can (19 oz/540 mL) pineapple tidbits, drained	1
6	medium yams, cooked, peeled and mashed	6
1/4 cup	brandy, divided	50 mL
2 tbsp	grated orange peel	25 mL
1/2 cup	brown sugar	125 mL
1 tsp	cinnamon	5 mL
1/2 tsp	cloves	2 mL
2 tbsp	Imperial Margarine	25 mL
1/2 cup	chopped pecans	125 mL

In a greased 8-cup (2 L) shallow casserole, layer half the pineapple and half the yams. Top with 2 tbsp (25 mL) brandy. Combine orange peel, brown sugar, cinnamon and cloves; top yams with half of this mixture. Repeat layers; dot top with margarine and sprinkle with pecans. Bake, uncovered, at 350°F (180°C) 30–40 minutes or until top is crusty.

Microwave: Assemble casserole as above. Heat at HIGH (100%) 10–12 minutes. Let stand, covered, 5 minutes.

Makes 8 servings.

TIP: Bake yams or sweet potatoes whole. Be sure to prick skin in several places and either wrap in aluminum foil or place a piece of foil under them in the oven to catch the syrupy drippings.

Calories per serving: 254   Vitamin C: Excellent

NUTTY YAM BAKE

Preparation: about 10 minutes   Cook: 30 minutes

Serve this sure winner for make-ahead preparation with a pork or ham roast and a green vegetable.

2	cans (19 oz/540 mL) yams, drained and mashed *or*	2
4	yams, cooked, peeled and mashed	4
1	pouch Lipton Golden Onion Soup	1
2	eggs, slightly beaten	2
1/2 cup	chopped pecans *or* walnuts	125 mL
1/4 cup	margarine *or* butter, melted	50 mL
1/4 cup	brown sugar	50 mL
1/2 tsp	ground cinnamon	2 mL
1/8 tsp	ground nutmeg	0.5 mL
	Flaked coconut (optional)	

In a large bowl, combine ingredients. Turn into a lightly greased 6-cup (1.5 L) casserole and top, if desired, with coconut. Bake, uncovered, at 350°F (180°C) 30 minutes or until heated through.

Makes approximately 8 servings.

Calories per serving: 224   Vitamin A: Excellent

ZUCCHINI FINGERS

Preparation: under 10 minutes   Cook: 20 minutes

Coating these zucchini fingers with salad dressing before dipping them into bread crumbs, gives a subtly different taste depending on the type of dressing used.

½ cup	dry bread crumbs	125 mL	In a small bowl, combine bread crumbs and
⅓ cup	Black Diamond Grated Parmesan Cheese	75 mL	cheese. Dip zucchini fingers in dressing then coat with bread crumb mixture. Place on a
2	medium zucchini, cut in 1 × 4-inch (2.5 × 10 cm) fingers	2	greased baking sheet and bake at 375°F (190°C) about 20 minutes or until crisp and golden.
½ cup	Country-Style Dressing (page 37)	125 mL	**Makes 2 main course or 4 appetizer servings.**

Calories per main course serving: 323   Vitamin C: Excellent   Calcium: Good

ZUCCHINI CUSTARD

Preparation: about 10 minutes   Cook: 55 minutes

Make Zucchini Custard ahead of time and serve it with Herbed Tomatoes (page 105) and baked ham for an easy oven meal.

1	medium onion, sliced	1
2 tbsp	margarine *or* butter, melted	25 mL
3	medium zucchini, cut in ½-inch (1 cm) slices	3
2 tsp	Lawry's Seasoned Salt	10 mL
½ tsp	Lawry's Seasoned Pepper	2 mL
6	eggs	6
1 cup	milk	250 mL
½ lb	Black Diamond Mozzarella Cheese, sliced	250 g

In a medium covered skillet, over medium-high heat, sauté onion in margarine about 5 minutes. Add zucchini, seasoned salt and seasoned pepper and sauté for about 5 minutes or until lightly browned. In a medium bowl, beat eggs and milk; stir in vegetable mixture. Pour into a greased 8-cup (2 L) oblong baking dish. Set dish in a pan of hot water. Bake, uncovered, at 300°F (150°C) 25 minutes. Top with cheese. Bake 25 minutes or until custard is firm.

Microwave: Sauté vegetables as above. Combine beaten eggs, milk and vegetables. Pour into a greased 8-cup (2 L) oblong dish. Heat at HIGH (100%) 2 minutes; stir. Heat at MEDIUM (50%) 4–6 minutes; stir, turn dish, heat 4–6 minutes or until almost set. Top with cheese; heat 2–3 minutes until cheese melts.

Makes 6–8 servings.

TIP: Carrots can be substituted for zucchini.

Calories per serving: 227   Calcium and vitamin C: Good

SEASONED VEGETABLE PLATTER

Preparation: 15 minutes   Cook: about 10 minutes

This is a convenient way to cook a variety of vegetables together at the same time. The colorful profusion of vegetables can be arranged on a serving dish and microwaved in minutes. Or they can be cooked in a steamer. Either way, this is a spectacular way to serve vegetables.

2	medium carrots, sliced diagonally	2
2 cups	broccoli florets	500 mL
2 cups	cauliflower florets	500 mL
1	medium zucchini, thinly sliced	1
½	red *or* green pepper, sliced	½
¼ lb	fresh mushrooms, sliced	125 g
1	tomato cut into 6 wedges (optional)	1
	or	
6	cherry tomatoes (optional) Seasoned Topping *or* Lemon Sauce (recipes follow)	6

Place vegetables and tomato on a steamer rack ½ inch (1 cm) above boiling water in a large saucepan. Cook, covered, until tender, about 10 minutes. Arrange on a platter (larger vegetables may be sliced in half but should still retain the identity of the full-sized vegetable). Drizzle Seasoned Topping of your choice over whole platter, or place a small dish of topping or Lemon Sauce on the side for dipping.

Microwave: On a large glass serving platter, arrange carrot slices around the outside; then broccoli and cauliflower. Arrange zucchini, pepper and mushrooms in center. Drizzle Seasoned Topping over vegetables. Cover with plastic wrap. Heat at HIGH (100%) 6–8 minutes or until tender-crisp; rotate once. If desired, arrange tomato wedges or cherry tomatoes on top of broccoli and cauliflower circle. Re-cover and heat at HIGH 1–2 minutes longer. Let stand 2 minutes.

Calories per serving: 43, without topping   Vitamins A and C: Excellent   Fiber: Good
Low fat

SEASONED TOPPINGS   Preparation: under 5 minutes

It only takes seconds to make these seasoned toppings, which will perk up the plainest vegetables.

Lemon Pepper:

¼ cup	margarine *or* butter	50 mL
2 tsp	Lawry's Lemon Pepper	10 mL

Garlic:

¼ cup	margarine *or* butter	50 mL
2 tsp	Lawry's Garlic Spread Concentrate	10 mL

Sherry:

¼ cup	margarine *or* butter	50 mL
1–2 tbsp	sherry	15–25 mL
Dash	pepper	Dash

Tarragon:

¼ cup	margarine *or* butter	50 mL
1 tbsp	tarragon	15 mL

In a small saucepan, melt margarine; stir in seasoning.

Microwave: In a 1-cup (250 mL) measure, melt margarine at HIGH (100%) 45–60 seconds; stir in seasoning.

Makes ¼ cup (50 mL).

LEMON SAUCE

This citrus sauce is a natural addition to vegetables or seafood.

¼ cup	Becel Margarine	50 mL
1 tbsp	lemon juice	15 mL
1 tbsp	chopped fresh parsley	15 mL
Dash	cayenne pepper *or* Tabasco sauce (optional)	Dash
¼ tsp	grated lemon rind	1 mL

Calories per 1 tbsp (15 mL): 44

In a small saucepan, melt margarine; stir in remaining ingredients.

Microwave: Combine all ingredients. Heat at HIGH (100%) 1–2 minutes.

Makes ½ cup (125 mL).

TIP: Fats absorb microwave energy and melt rapidly. If you use the microwave oven for this sauce, make it in the dish you will use for serving.

GARDEN LASAGNA

Preparation: about 10 minutes   Cook: 30 minutes

When you grow tired of "the same old thing," try a meatless entrée like Garden Lasagna as one way of varying your menu.

1	pouch Lipton Onion Soup	1
1	can (7½ oz/213 mL) tomato sauce	1
2 cups	milk	500 mL
3 tbsp	all-purpose flour	45 mL
2 tbsp	margarine *or* butter	25 mL
1	clove garlic, minced	1
½ cup	Black Diamond Grated Parmesan Cheese	125 mL
8	lasagna noodles, cooked to tender but firm stage	8
1	package (300 g) frozen chopped broccoli, thawed and drained	1
1	package (300 g) frozen mixed vegetables	1
1 cup	grated Black Diamond Mozzarella Cheese	250 mL

In a medium saucepan, combine soup mix, tomato sauce, milk, flour, margarine and garlic. Cook, stirring, until smooth and thickened, about 5 minutes; add Parmesan cheese. In a lightly greased oblong baking pan, spread ½ cup (125 mL) sauce. Layer with 4 lasagna noodles, drained vegetables, Mozzarella cheese, half remaining sauce, 4 noodles and top with remaining sauce. Bake at 350°F (180°C) 30 minutes. Let stand 10 minutes.

Microwave: In a medium bowl, combine soup mix, tomato sauce, milk, flour, margarine and garlic. Heat at HIGH (100%) 8–9 minutes; stir occasionally until smooth and thickened. Add cheese. Assemble casserole as above. Heat at HIGH 10 minutes; rotate dish. Heat 5 minutes. Let stand 10 minutes.

Makes 5–6 servings.

TIP: Can be prepared ahead and frozen.

Calories per serving: 566   Calcium; thiamin; vitamins A and C: Excellent   Iron: Good

FRESH VEGETABLE CASSEROLE

Preparation: about 10 minutes   Cook: about 30 minutes

One year we grew zucchini in our garden. It became an ongoing challenge to find as many ways as possible to use our bumper crop. This recipe was a delicious discovery.

3	medium zucchini, thinly sliced	3
½ cup	chopped onion	125 mL
2 tbsp	Becel Margarine, melted	25 mL
1	container (500 g) low-fat cottage cheese	1
1 tsp	basil	5 mL
½ tsp	oregano	2 mL
2	tomatoes, sliced	2
⅓ cup	Black Diamond Grated Parmesan Cheese	75 mL

In a large skillet, sauté zucchini and chopped onion in margarine. In a blender, cream cottage cheese, basil and oregano. In a 6-cup (1.5 L) lightly greased casserole, arrange alternate layers of zucchini, cottage cheese and tomato slices. Top with cheese. Bake, uncovered, at 350°F (180°C) 25–30 minutes.

Makes 6 servings.

Calories per serving: 133   Vitamin C: Excellent   Vitamin A: Good

TERIYAKI STIR-FRIED VEGETABLES

Preparation: about 10 minutes   Cook: about 5 minutes

One of the delights of stir-fried vegetables is their crunchy texture and bright color. As well, vegetables retain nutrients when cooked by this method.

1 tbsp	brown sugar	15 mL
2 tbsp	EACH: dry sherry, soy sauce	25 mL
½ tsp	ginger	2 mL
1	pouch Lipton Golden Onion Soup	1
⅛ tsp	Lawry's Seasoned Pepper	0.5 mL
1	clove garlic, minced	1
2 tbsp	vegetable oil	25 mL
4 cups	sliced Chinese cabbage *or* green cabbage	1 L
2 cups	snow peas, trimmed and halved	500 mL
½ cup	sliced green onions	125 mL
1	can (10 oz/284 mL) water chestnuts, drained and sliced	1

In a small bowl, prepare sauce by combining brown sugar, sherry, soy sauce, ginger, soup mix, seasoned pepper and garlic. In a large skillet or wok, over high heat, heat oil; add vegetables and sauce; stir-fry 5–7 minutes or until tender-crisp. Serve immediately.

Makes 5–6 servings.

TIP: The secret of stir-fry cooking is to keep the heat high and the food in motion. Chopsticks are the most efficient utensils for stirring food in a wok. If you don't have a wok, a large skillet can be used.

Calories per serving: 147   Fiber; vitamins A and C: Excellent   Iron: Good

CREAMED VEGETARIAN'S DELIGHT

Preparation: about 10 minutes   Cook: 10 minutes

This multicolored vegetable mixture can be served over rice or noodles for a vegetarian meal.

1 cup	broccoli pieces	250 mL
2 cups	thinly sliced carrots	500 mL
1 cup	sliced fresh mushrooms	250 mL
2	medium onions, cut in eighths	2
½ cup	vegetable oil	125 mL
1	pouch Lipton Bon Appétit Cream of Asparagus Soup	1
1 cup	water	250 mL
½ cup	sour cream	125 mL
	Hot cooked rice *or* noodles	

In a medium skillet, stir-fry each of the vegetables separately in oil until tender-crisp. Set aside and keep warm. Meanwhile, in a medium saucepan, combine soup mix with water, bring to a boil, reduce heat and simmer 5 minutes, stirring constantly. Add sour cream, combine with stir-fried vegetables and heat to serving temperature. Serve over rice or noodles.

Makes 4 servings.

Calories per serving: 393, without rice or noodles   Vitamins A and C: Excellent   Fiber: Good

YOLK-FREE HOLLANDAISE

Preparation: about 5 minutes

To give your heart a lasting chance, it's wise to reduce cholesterol. This Hollandaise recipe omits the egg yolks.

2	egg whites	2
½ tsp	dry mustard	2 mL
¼ tsp	salt	1 mL
Dash	cayenne pepper	Dash
¼ cup	fresh lemon juice	50 mL
¾ cup	Becel Margarine	175 mL

In a blender, place egg whites, mustard, salt, cayenne pepper and lemon juice. Blend on low speed for a few seconds. In a small saucepan, heat margarine until bubbly. Add slowly to egg white mixture while blending at high speed, until thickened. Serve immediately over hot vegetables (e.g. asparagus, broccoli, cauliflower).

Makes approximately 1¼ cups (300 mL).

TIP: Can be refrigerated and reheated.

Calories per 1 tbsp (15 mL): 63

BREADS, MUFFINS AND COOKIES

You can send quick loving messages with breads, muffins and cookies — they are old-fashioned treats that are today's comfort foods. When new people move into the neighborhood, they'll feel a special welcome if you take them a basket of warm muffins. When a friend is sick, let her or him know you care by taking over squares or a loaf of tea bread, wrapped in plastic wrap and tied with ribbon. When sons or daughters are away at university, there is nothing they appreciate more than care packages of their favorite cookies. (Pack them in unsalted popcorn so they receive cookies instead of crumbs.) Of course, these treats are particularly suited to holiday giving. They always give a personal message that is special.

QUICK SEASONING TIPS

The scent of sweet spices—ginger, nutmeg and cinnamon—throughout the house is one of the delights of baking. For the freshest spice flavors, use a grinder and prepare spices like nutmeg and cardamom as you use them. For optimum flavor, a good rule of thumb for preground spices is to use them within one year. If the ground spices in your cupboard seem to have lost their aroma and taste, discard them and buy fresh supplies.

CREATIVE DECORATING TIPS

Bread and muffins are such wholesome foods that they only need simple decorating—or none at all. Glaze bread and sprinkle on sesame seeds or poppy seeds. Top muffins with grated peel, cinnamon sugar or date pieces. However, you can use your imaginative decorating with cookies, especially at holiday season. Decorate cookies by dipping half the cookie into chocolate or thin icing, or dab the cookie with chocolate and top with a nut meat. Keep a stock of colored sugars, chocolate shot or sprinkles, chocolate chips, chopped nuts, halved or whole nut meats, candied fruit, coconut and gumdrops on your supply shelf. Use them in countless creative ways to decorate your cookies and cakes.

SPICED TEA BREAD

Preparation: about 15 minutes   Cook: 50 minutes

This loaf is delicious for a snack or for tea. It is particularly suitable for gifts. Consider making a variety of tea breads in small loaf pans. Wrap and freeze them. When you're ready to give them away, tie a selection together with a wide ribbon and a sprig of holly for Christmas or a flower for another special occasion.

⅓ cup	Imperial Margarine	75 mL
1 cup	sugar	250 mL
2	eggs	2
1 cup	shredded carrot *or* zucchini *or* mashed banana	250 mL
⅓ cup	water	75 mL
1½ cups + 2 tbsp	all-purpose flour	400 mL
1 tsp	baking soda	5 mL
¼ tsp	Blue Ribbon Double Action Baking Powder	1 mL
½ tsp	EACH: salt, cinnamon, cloves	2 mL
⅓ cup	chopped almonds	75 mL

In a medium bowl, cream margarine and gradually add sugar; beat until light and fluffy. Add eggs, carrot and water; mix thoroughly. In another mixing bowl, combine dry ingredients; add to creamed mixture; stir well. Stir in almonds. Spoon batter into a 9 × 5-inch (2 L) loaf pan greased only on the bottom. Bake at 350°F (180°C) 50 minutes or until a wooden pick inserted in center comes out clean. Cool in pan 10 minutes; remove and let cool completely.

Makes 1 loaf.

TIP: To keep nuts or fruit from sinking to the bottom of the batter, toss them in flour or sugar first.

Calories per slice: 204   Vitamin A: Excellent

SHORTCUT CHEESE BREAD

Preparation: about 10 minutes   Cook: about 20 minutes

This recipe uses not one, but two shortcuts in the preparation — soup mix and tea biscuit baking mix. Make ahead and freeze for another shortcut. To serve, unwrap and place in a 450°F (230°C) oven; turn off the oven. Leave for ten minutes for a fresh-tasting loaf with a crispy crust.

1	pouch Lipton Onion *or* Onion-Mushroom Soup	1
¼ cup	vegetable oil	50 mL
⅔ cup	milk	150 mL
2	eggs, slightly beaten	2
3 cups	variety biscuit mix	750 mL
¼ cup	finely chopped fresh parsley	50 mL
½ cup	grated Black Diamond Cheddar Cheese	125 mL

In a small bowl, combine soup mix, oil, milk and eggs. In a medium bowl, combine baking mix and parsley. Add liquid ingredients to dry; stir together to make a soft dough. Spread evenly in a greased deep 9-inch (1.5 L) round baking pan. Bake at 400°F (200°C) 20–25 minutes or until done. Sprinkle with grated cheese, and warm just before serving. May be frozen.

Makes 1 round loaf.

Calories per slice: 163

CINNAMON PINWHEEL COFFEE CAKE

Preparation: under 15 minutes   Cook: 20 minutes

For a leisurely brunch or coffee klatch, this type of cinnamon-flavored sweet bread is a perfect accompaniment to coffee.

2/3 cup	Monarch Cinnamon Spread	150 mL
1/2 cup	packed brown sugar	125 mL
1 tbsp	water	15 mL
12	walnut or cherry halves	12
2 cups	all-purpose flour	500 mL
1/4 cup	sugar	50 mL
1 tbsp	Blue Ribbon Double Action Baking Powder	15 mL
1/2 tsp	salt	2 mL
1/2 cup	hard Imperial Margarine	125 mL
3/4 cup	milk	175 mL
1/2 cup	chopped nuts	125 mL

In a small bowl, combine cinnamon spread and brown sugar. Place half in a greased 8-inch (2 L) square pan; blend in water. Bake at 375°F (190°C) 1 minute or until cinnamon mixture has softened; blend well. Arrange walnuts in rows on cinnamon mixture. In a medium bowl, combine dry ingredients. Cut in margarine with a pastry blender or 2 knives until mixture is crumbly. Stir in milk with a fork until it forms a dough. Place on a lightly floured surface and knead gently until smooth. Roll into a 9 × 12-inch (22 × 30 cm) rectangle. Spread remaining cinnamon mixture and chopped nuts evenly over dough. Roll up jelly roll style from the long side. Cut into twelve 1-inch (2.5 cm) pieces. Place each pinwheel slice on top of each walnut in baking pan. Bake at 375°F (190°C) 20 minutes. Turn out, upside down, immediately onto a serving plate. Serve warm. May be frozen.

Makes 1 coffee cake.

Calories per serving: 297

HONEY AND CINNAMON DROP SCONE BISCUITS

Preparation: under 10 minutes   Cook: about 10 minutes

Traditional scones are rolled and cut. These drop scones are made more quickly.

2 cups	all-purpose flour	500 mL
2 tsp	Blue Ribbon Double Action Baking Powder	10 mL
1/2 tsp	EACH: salt, nutmeg	2 mL
1 tsp	cinnamon	5 mL
1/2 cup	hard Imperial Margarine	125 mL
1/2 cup	raisins	125 mL
1/4 cup	milk	50 mL
1	egg	1
1/2 cup	liquid honey	125 mL

In a large bowl, combine dry ingredients; cut in margarine with a pastry blender or 2 knives. In a small bowl, combine raisins, milk, egg and honey. Add liquid ingredients to dry; stir with a fork to form a dough. On an ungreased baking sheet, drop large spoonfuls 2 inches (5 cm) apart. Bake at 400°F (200°C) 10–15 minutes or until golden. May be frozen.

Makes 1 1/2–2 dozen scones.

Calories per scone: 110

TEA-TIME SCONES

Preparation: about 10 minutes   Cook: about 12 minutes

Make traditional tea-time scones even better with the addition of ginger and apricots. If you'd rather serve them for brunch or lunch, make the cheese and oregano variation.

1¼ cups	all-purpose flour	300 mL
1½ tsp	Blue Ribbon Double Action Baking Powder	7 mL
2 tbsp	icing sugar	25 mL
½ tsp	powdered ginger (optional)	2 mL
¼ cup	chopped dried apricots	50 mL
¼ cup	Becel Margarine, melted	50 mL
½ cup	skim milk	125 mL

In a medium bowl, combine dry ingredients and apricots; add margarine and milk; stir with a fork to form a soft dough. Place on a lightly floured surface and knead gently until smooth. Roll to ½-inch (1 cm) thickness; cut into 2-inch (5 cm) rounds. Place on ungreased baking sheet. Bake at 425°F (220°C) 12–15 minutes or until golden brown. May be frozen.

Makes 10-12 scones.

Calories per scone: 87

VARIATION

Meal-Time Scones: Replace ginger and apricots with 2 tbsp (25 mL) Black Diamond Grated Parmesan Cheese and 1 tsp (5 mL) dried oregano.

APPLE-BRAN BREAKFAST MUFFINS

Preparation: about 10 minutes   Cook: about 20 minutes

Muffins are great for the hurry-up cook because they are quickly made and freeze well. Before freezing, cool them completely and wrap securely. They can be stored frozen for three months.

1½ cups	wheat bran cereal	375 mL
¾ cup	skim milk	175 mL
¼ cup	Becel Margarine, melted	50 mL
¼ cup	molasses	50 mL
1½ cups	coarsely grated apple	375 mL
½ cup	EACH: whole wheat and all-purpose flour	125 mL
½–1 tsp	nutmeg	2–5 mL
2 tbsp	toasted wheat germ	25 mL
1½ tsp	Blue Ribbon Double Action Baking Powder	7 mL
½ tsp	baking soda	2 mL
2	large egg whites, stiffly beaten	2

In a medium bowl, combine bran and milk; let stand 3 minutes. Stir in margarine, molasses and apple. In another bowl, combine dry ingredients; stir into bran mixture just until mixed. Fold in beaten egg whites; spoon batter evenly into 12 greased large muffin cups. Bake at 350°F (180°C) 20–25 minutes or until done.

Makes 12 muffins.

TIP: Muffins are easier to remove if allowed to remain in the pan for a few minutes after baking.

Calories per muffin: 127   Iron and thiamin: Good

RHUBARB ORANGE MUFFINS

Preparation: about 10 minutes   Cook: about 15 minutes

Just imagine the aroma of these muffins, with their tangy blend of rhubarb and orange, baking for breakfast. Or serve them as snacks to satisfy those between-meal cravings.

2 cups	all-purpose flour	500 mL
½ cup	sugar	125 mL
1½ tsp	Blue Ribbon Double Action Baking Powder	7 mL
½ tsp	EACH: baking soda, salt	2 mL
1	egg	1
½ cup	melted Country Crock Margarine	125 mL
½ cup	orange juice	125 mL
2 tsp	grated orange peel	10 mL
1½ cups	finely chopped rhubarb	375 mL

In a large bowl, combine dry ingredients. In a medium bowl, beat egg, margarine, orange juice and peel until well blended; add rhubarb. Pour liquid ingredients into dry ingredients; stir just until mixed. Spoon batter evenly into 12 greased medium muffin cups. Bake at 400°F (200°C) 15–20 minutes or until golden. May be frozen.

Makes 12 muffins.

TIP: Keep a small container of margarine in the refrigerator with a plastic sandwich bag inside. To grease a baking or muffin pan, just slip the bag over your hand and grease away. Return the bag to the container for the next time.

Calories per muffin: 158

SEASONAL FRESH FRUIT MUFFINS

Preparation: about 10 minutes   Cook: about 15 minutes

These delicious muffins contain 50 percent less fat and 50 percent fewer calories when you use Country Crock Margarine. However, only cook with it in tested recipes. Its high moisture content requires adjustment of the recipe ingredients.

2 cups	all-purpose flour	500 mL
½ cup	sugar	125 mL
⅓ cup	dry skim milk powder	75 mL
1 tbsp	Blue Ribbon Double Action Baking Powder	15 mL
½ tsp	salt	2 mL
1	egg	1
½ cup	melted Country Crock Margarine	125 mL
½ cup	water *or* skim milk	125 mL
2 tsp	lemon juice	10 mL
½ tsp	grated lemon peel	2 mL
1 cup	fresh fruit, chopped or sliced (strawberries, raspberries, peaches, nectarines, blueberries)	250 mL

In a large bowl, combine dry ingredients. In a medium bowl, beat egg, margarine, water, lemon juice and peel until well blended; add fruit. Pour liquid ingredients into dry ingredients; stir just until mixed. Spoon batter evenly into 12 greased medium muffin cups. Bake at 400°F (200°C) 15–20 minutes or until golden. May be frozen.

Makes 12 muffins.

TIPS: 1. For raspberry, peach or nectarine muffins, replace lemon juice and peel with ½ tsp (2 mL) mace. 2. Do not double recipe. Make separate batters when using different fruits.

Calories per muffin: 166   Vitamin C: Good

HAM AND CHEDDAR MUFFINS

Preparation: under 10 minutes   Cook: about 15 minutes

Ham and Cheddar Muffins are a welcome change for a luncheon or brunch. Serve with soup, some vegetable sticks, milk and fresh fruit for a nutritious meal.

2 cups	variety biscuit mix	500 mL
2 tbsp	sugar	25 mL
1	can (6.5 oz/184 g) Puritan Flaked Ham, flaked with a fork	1
1½ cups	grated Black Diamond Cheddar Cheese	375 mL
1	egg, slightly beaten	1
1 cup	milk	250 mL

In a medium bowl, combine baking mix, sugar, ham and cheese. Stir in egg and milk with a fork just until combined. Spoon batter evenly into 12 greased medium muffin cups. Bake at 400°F (200°C) 15–20 minutes. Serve warm or reheat. May be frozen.

Makes 12 muffins.

TIPS: 1. Keep muffins or bread hot longer by lining your basket under the napkin with aluminum foil. 2. For larger muffins, add extra batter to each muffin cup.

Calories per muffin: 192

CARROT COOKIES

Preparation: about 10 minutes   Cook: about 10 minutes

Rolled cookies always have a delicious, old-fashioned taste that reminds me of the sugar cookies my grandmother used to make. She would serve them warm from the oven. On special occasions, she would sandwich them together with a sweetened filling.

½ cup	Imperial Margarine, softened	125 mL
1 cup	brown sugar	250 mL
1	egg	1
1½ cups	finely shredded carrots	375 mL
2½ cups	all-purpose flour	625 mL
1½ tsp	cinnamon	7 mL
1 tsp	Blue Ribbon Double Action Baking Powder	5 mL
½ tsp	salt	2 mL
¼ tsp	nutmeg	1 mL
	Cream Cheese Frosting (recipe follows)	

In a large bowl, cream margarine with sugar until light and fluffy; beat in egg and carrots. In a medium bowl, combine remaining ingredients. Gradually stir into creamed mixture, blending well after each addition. Cover and chill at least 2 hours. On a well-floured board, roll dough ¼ inch (6 mm) thick; cut with a round cookie cutter; place on ungreased baking sheets. Bake at 400°F (200°C) 10–15 minutes. Cool completely. May be frozen. Spread with Cream Cheese Frosting.

Makes approximately 2½–3 dozen cookies.

CREAM CHEESE FROSTING

1	package (250 g) cream cheese, softened	1
3 cups	icing sugar	750 mL

In a medium bowl, cream cheese with icing sugar. Food color and flavor extracts may be added, if desired.

TIP: Dip cookie cutters into vegetable oil or flour before using for a cleaner cut with less sticking.

Calories per cookie: 83, unfrosted; 148, frosted

CHEESY ONION TWISTS

Preparation: about 5 minutes   Cook: 10 minutes

It's easy to welcome your family or guests with the smell of baking bread when you make these quickly prepared rolls.

1	package (235 g) refrigerated crescent rolls	1
1 tbsp	margarine *or* butter, melted	15 mL
2 tsp	minced green onion	10 mL
2 tbsp	grated Black Diamond Cheddar Cheese	25 mL
	Additional melted margarine *or* butter	
	Dill weed, caraway *or* poppy seeds	

On a cutting board, unroll crescent rolls in a long strip. Brush with margarine, top with green onion and cheese. Fold lengthwise into thirds. Cut into four strips crosswise; twist and place on a greased baking sheet. Brush with margarine; top with dill weed, caraway or poppy seeds. Bake at 425°F (220°C) 10 minutes. May be frozen.

Makes 4 rolls.

Calories per roll: 251

ORANGE SHORTBREAD

Preparation: about 10 minutes   Cook: 20 minutes

If you would like to have a variety of shortbread and cookies at Christmas, but don't have much time to bake, organize a cookie-swap party. You and five friends bake six dozen cookies, then get together to exchange and sample them. When it's time to leave, everyone will have a fast "fun" start on holiday baking and dozens of cookies for entertaining.

1 cup	Becel Margarine	250 mL
½ cup	icing sugar	125 mL
1¾ cups	all-purpose flour	425 mL
¼ cup	rice flour	50 mL
	Grated rind of 1 orange	

In a medium bowl, cream margarine until light and fluffy. Add sugar gradually, beating constantly. Combine flours, add orange rind and stir into batter. On a lightly floured board, pat dough to ¼-inch (5 mm) thickness; cut with a 2-inch (5 cm) cookie cutter. Place on greased baking sheets. Bake at 325°F (160°C) 20 minutes or until golden brown. May be frozen.

Makes about 3 dozen cookies.

Calories per cookie: 86

VARIATIONS

Almond Shortbread: Replace orange rind with ⅔ cup (150 mL) toasted, chopped almonds; stir into batter.

Coconut Shortbread: Replace orange rind with lemon rind; add ⅔ cup (150 mL) unsweetened coconut to flours and stir into batter. Top cut-out cookies with 2 tbsp (25 mL) each: unsweetened coconut and granulated sugar before baking.

Ginger Shortbread: Replace grated orange rind with ¼ cup (50 mL) finely minced candied ginger *or* 2 tsp (10 mL) ground ginger. Decorate cut-out cookies with slivers of candied ginger before baking.

TIP: This shortbread recipe has been adapted for Becel Margarine, so you can indulge in this Christmas treat even if you are watching saturated fats in your diet.

CHUNKY CHOCOLATE SLAB SQUARES

Preparation: about 15 minutes   Cook: about 20 minutes

Among the most convenient cookie recipes are those you can make in slabs and cut into squares. It saves so much time!

¾ cup	chunky peanut butter	175 mL
¼ cup	Imperial Margarine, softened	50 mL
1 cup	EACH: granulated sugar, firmly packed brown sugar	250 mL
2	eggs	2
1 tsp	vanilla extract	5 mL
2½ cups	all-purpose flour	625 mL
2 tsp	baking soda	10 mL
¾ tsp	salt	3 mL
4	squares semi-sweet chocolate, chopped into small chunks	4

In a large bowl, cream peanut butter and margarine. Gradually add sugar; cream until light and fluffy. Beat in eggs and vanilla. In a medium bowl, combine flour, soda and salt; stir into creamed mixture. Stir in chocolate chunks. Press mixture into a greased jelly roll pan. Bake at 350°F (180°C) 20–25 minutes or until golden brown. Cut into squares immediately. May be frozen.

Makes 2½–3 dozen squares.

Calories per square: 139

SESAME FINGERS

Preparation: about 15 minutes   Cook: 20 minutes

Until I found this recipe I used to buy small packages of sesame bars. These faintly sweet, nutty-flavored Sesame Fingers are nutritious additions to bag lunches.

⅓ cup	Becel Margarine	75 mL
½ cup	EACH: brown sugar, honey	125 mL
2 cups	rolled oats	500 mL
1 cup	EACH: unprocessed bran, sunflower seeds	250 mL
1 cup	pecans, chopped	250 mL
½ cup	EACH: walnuts, chopped, and toasted sesame seeds	125 mL

In a small saucepan over low heat, melt margarine; add sugar and honey and stir until sugar has dissolved. Bring to a boil; gently simmer for 5 minutes; cool slightly. In a large bowl, combine remaining ingredients. Gradually stir in margarine mixture. Press mixture into a greased 11 × 7-inch (2 L) jelly roll pan. Bake at 350°F (180°C) 15 minutes or until golden brown. Cool and cut into fingers.

Makes approximately 3½ dozen.

Calories per serving: 118

VARIATIONS

Replace pecans with 1½ cups (375 mL) mixed dried fruit *or* 1 cup (250 mL) chopped dates.

CHEESY APRICOT SQUARES

Preparation: under 10 minutes   Cook: about 30 minutes

This is one of those versatile recipes that can be varied with your mood or what you happen to have in the cupboard. Instead of apricot jam, try strawberry or raspberry jam, grape or apple jelly.

¼ cup	hard Imperial Margarine	50 mL
1 cup	grated Black Diamond Mozzarella *or* Cheddar Cheese	250 mL
¼ cup	sugar	50 mL
1½ cups	all-purpose flour	375 mL
1 tsp	Blue Ribbon Double Action Baking Powder	5 mL
1 cup	apricot jam	250 mL

In a medium bowl, combine margarine, cheese, sugar, flour and baking powder with a pastry blender or 2 knives. Press three-quarters of the mixture on bottom of a greased 8-inch (2 L) square pan. Spread with jam. Sprinkle remaining mixture on top. Bake at 350°F (180°C) 30–40 minutes or until browned on top. Cool and cut into small squares. May be frozen.

Makes approximately 36 squares.

TIP: If baking powder picks up moisture from the air, it loses its leavening power. To test the powder before using, mix 1 tsp (5 mL) in ⅓ cup (75 mL) hot water. If it bubbles furiously, the powder is still active and useable.

Calories per square: 82

UNBAKED CHRISTMAS COOKIES

Preparation: about 10 minutes   Chill: 25 minutes

These cookies can be rolled into balls or patted into a pan and cut into bars when set. Whatever your time allows!

3	pouches Knox Unflavoured Gelatine	3
1 cup	orange, apple *or* pineapple juice	250 mL
1 cup	chopped candied fruit	250 mL
1 cup	chopped red and green cherries	250 mL
2 cups	granola	500 mL
½ cup	EACH: flaked coconut, chopped nuts	125 mL

In a medium saucepan, sprinkle gelatine over juice; let stand 1 minute. Over low heat, stir until gelatine is completely dissolved, about 5 minutes. Stir in remaining ingredients; mix well. Chill 10–15 minutes until partially set. Roll into 1-inch (2.5 cm) balls, chill again until firm; or pat mixture into an oblong pan.

Makes 3–4 dozen cookies.

Calories per cookie: 71

VARIATION

Rocky Road Cookies: Reduce granola to 1 cup (250 mL); add ½ cup (125 mL) chocolate chips and ½ cup (125 mL) miniature marshmallows.

OLD-FASHIONED FUDGE

Preparation: about 15 minutes   Chill: about 1½ hours

Gelatine gives a smooth, creamy texture to this old-fashioned fudge. One of our staff made it at home with her daughter, who took it to a grade three French Immersion class party. Her classmates agreed unanimously that it was a *très bon* fudge.

1	pouch Knox Unflavoured Gelatine	1
3 cups	sugar	750 mL
1 cup	milk	250 mL
½ cup	light corn syrup	125 mL
3	squares unsweetened chocolate	3
1¼ cups	margarine *or* butter	300 mL
2 tsp	vanilla extract	10 mL
1 cup	coarsely chopped walnuts (optional)	250 mL

In a medium saucepan, combine gelatine, sugar, milk, corn syrup, chocolate and margarine. Cook over medium heat, stirring frequently, to 238°F (112°C) on candy thermometer or soft ball stage. Remove from heat; pour into a large bowl. Stir in vanilla; cool 25 minutes. Beat with a wooden spoon until candy thickens. Spread in a lightly greased 8-inch (2 L) square pan and refrigerate until firm enough to cut into squares. May be frozen.

Makes 5 dozen squares.

TIP: Soft ball stage in candy making can be determined when a little syrup in cold water forms a soft ball that flattens when removed from the water.

Calories per serving: 105

RAISIN AND PEANUT BLOX

Preparation: about 10 minutes   Chill: 1–2 hours

Knox is famous for easy confections called Knox Blox.

3	pouches Knox Unflavoured Gelatine	3
⅓ cup	sugar	75 mL
1½ cups	apple juice	375 mL
½ cup	whipping cream	125 mL
½ tsp	EACH: cinnamon, vanilla extract	2 mL
½ cup	raisins	125 mL
⅓ cup	finely chopped peanuts	75 mL

In a medium saucepan, combine gelatine, sugar and juice. Stir, over low heat, until gelatine is completely dissolved, about 5 minutes. Stir in cream, cinnamon and vanilla. Chill, stirring occasionally, until mixture is consistency of unbeaten egg whites. Fold in raisins and peanuts. Turn into a lightly greased 8-inch (2 L) square pan; chill until firm. Cut into 1-inch (2.5 cm) squares.

Makes approximately 5 dozen blox.

Calories per blox: 24   Low fat

Clockwise: Red Rose Tea; Seasonal Fresh Fruit Muffins (page 117); Spiced Tea Bread (page 114); Cinnamon Pinwheel Coffee Cake (page 115)

MOCK CHOCOLATE RUM TRUFFLES

Preparation: about 15 minutes

Everyone loves truffles. You'll love them even more when you can make them with fewer calories.

3	eggs	3
¼ cup	water	50 mL
2 tbsp	light rum	25 mL
	or	
1 tsp	rum extract	5 mL
1 tbsp	frozen orange juice concentrate, thawed	15 mL
26	packets low-calorie sugar substitute (e.g. Equal)	26
⅓ cup	unsweetened cocoa	75 mL
1⅓ cups	fine dry bread crumbs	325 mL

In a medium bowl, beat eggs, water, rum and orange juice until thick and lemon-colored, 5–7 minutes. Gradually add sugar substitute. Fold in cocoa and bread crumbs. (Mixture will become very dense.) Shape rounded spoonfuls into small balls. Let stand at room temperature until outsides are dry. Refrigerate in airtight container. May be frozen.

Makes 2½–3 dozen truffles.

Calories per truffle: 29   Low fat

CHOCOLATE BROWNIES

Preparation: about 15 minutes   Cook: 20 minutes

A calorie-reduced luscious brownie made with cocoa and low-fat Country Crock Margarine. Serve unfrosted or frosted with a Low-Fat Vanilla Frosting.

¾ cup	all-purpose flour	175 mL
½ tsp	baking powder	2 mL
¼ tsp	salt	1 mL
½ cup	EACH: Country Crock Margarine, melted, and cocoa	125 mL
¾ cup	granulated sugar	175 mL
2	eggs	2
½ tsp	vanilla extract	2 mL
½ cup	chopped nuts (optional) Calorie-Reduced Frosting (page 131)	125 mL

In a small bowl, combine flour, baking powder and salt. In a medium bowl, cream margarine, cocoa and sugar; beat in eggs one at a time; add vanilla. Fold in dry ingredients and nuts. Spread batter into an 8-inch (2 L) pan coated with non-stick vegetable spray. Bake at 350°F (180°C) about 20 minutes. Cool and frost if desired.

Makes 15 servings.

Calories per serving: 133 unfrosted; 182 frosted

Clockwise: Herbal Sorbet (page 139); Chocolate Cake with Luscious Cappucino Frosting (page 130); Fruit Flan with Easy Dessert Glaze (page 126)

DESSERTS

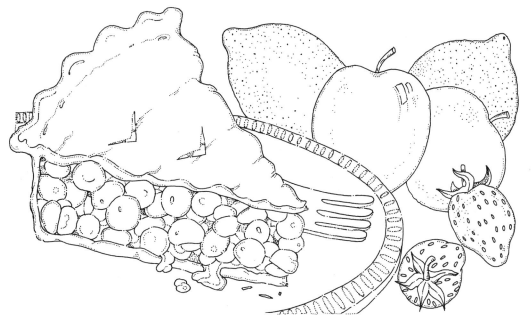

When you make some of these quick dessert recipes, let some of the decorating suggestions given throughout this section spark your imagination. You'll find out just how easy it is to turn a simple dessert into a spectacular one.

QUICK SEASONING TIPS

In baking, use vanilla sugar for a flavoring shortcut. Prepare simply by storing a vanilla bean in a tightly covered jar of granulated sugar. Add it to whipping cream, egg whites, custard, meringues and puddings. If you prefer vanilla extract, it's also simple to make. Place a vanilla bean in a small jar, add vodka or brandy and store in a cool place for a month before using. More variety can be added to recipes using other flavoring extracts, and be sure to experiment with spices, too. A good basic recipe for a cake, frosting, pudding or ice cream can be subtly changed with the addition of a spice, some orange, lemon or lime peel, or by changing the liquid from milk to fruit juice, coffee or liqueurs.

CREATIVE DECORATING TIPS

Take a simple spice cake and decorate with Luscious Cappucino Frosting (page 130) and pecans. You can sprinkle the top with chopped nuts and, if you like, press whole pecan meats around the edge. For a birthday celebration, press about five pecans into the center of the cake to form a flower and use it as a candle holder.

One of my favorite herbs, mint, is an instant decoration for desserts. For instance, serve the Strawberries in Chocolate Cups (page 129) with glazed strawberry garnishes and mint leaves for a sensational dessert. Make up parfaits of Knox Ice Cream (page 138) and garnish with small mint leaves and stemmed cherries. Or, use mint as a finishing touch to a cantaloupe basket of fresh fruit.

EASY DESSERT GLAZE

Preparation: about 5 minutes   Chill: about 1 hour

There's nothing that adds more sparkling glamor to a dessert than a glaze—use it on a fresh fruit flan, pie or tarts. It's easily made in five minutes with gelatine.

1	pouch Knox Unflavoured Gelatine	1
¼ cup	EACH: cold water, boiling water	50 mL
1 tbsp	EACH: liquid honey, lemon juice	15 mL

In a small bowl, sprinkle gelatine over cold water; let stand 3–4 minutes. Add boiling water; stir constantly until gelatine is completely dissolved. Stir in remaining ingredients. Chill 15–20 minutes, stirring occasionally, until mixture is consistency of unbeaten egg whites. Carefully spoon glaze over surface to cover; chill until set.

Makes enough glaze for a 10-inch (25 cm) flan or pie shell.

TIP: If liquid honey crystallizes, remove the lid and place the jar in a saucepan filled with several inches of hot water. Leave until honey melts. For a quicker method, warm honey in a microwave oven.

Calories per 1 tbsp (15 mL): 12   Low fat

RASPBERRY TRIFLE

Preparation: about 45 minutes   Chill: 3 hours

When you want a spectacular dessert for a dinner party, remember this light, unusual variation of an English Trifle. It is always popular with my family and guests.

1	9-inch (23 cm) angel food or sponge cake, cut into small cubes	1
¾ cup	cream sherry, divided	175 mL
1	package (425g) frozen sweetened raspberries, thawed and drained (reserve syrup)	1
1	pouch Knox Unflavoured Gelatine	1
¼ cup	sugar	50 mL
3	egg yolks	3
2 cups	milk, divided	500 mL
½ cup	whipping cream, whipped	125 mL
½ cup	slivered almonds, toasted	125 mL
1 tbsp	cornstarch	15 mL
	Water	

In a large bowl, sprinkle cake cubes with mixture of ½ cup (125 mL) sherry and ½ cup (125 mL) reserved raspberry syrup; toss gently. In a medium saucepan, combine gelatine with sugar; beat in egg yolks and ½ cup (125 mL) milk. Cook and stir over low heat until gelatine is completely dissolved, about 5 minutes. Stir in remaining sherry and milk. Pour into a large bowl and chill, stirring occasionally, until mixture mounds slightly when dropped from a spoon. Fold in whipped cream, then raspberries. In a large glass serving or punch bowl, layer one-third cake cubes, one-third raspberry mixture and one-third almonds; repeat twice. Chill until set, about 3 hours. Meanwhile, in a small saucepan, combine cornstarch and remaining syrup mixed with enough water to equal 1 cup (250 mL). Stir over medium heat until mixture thickens and clears; chill. Serve raspberry sauce over Trifle.

Makes approximately 8 servings.

Calories per serving: 481   Fiber: Good   Vitamin C and calcium: Good

GINGERBREAD CAKE WITH FRESH FRUIT SAUCE

Preparation: about 10 minutes   Cook: about 35 minutes

Combining Rhubarb Sauce with Gingerbread gives a spring lift to a winter dessert. By using other fresh or frozen fruit, you can make gingerbread a dessert for all seasons.

2 cups	all-purpose flour	500 mL
1/3 cup	sugar	75 mL
1 1/2 tsp	baking soda	7 mL
1/2 tsp	salt	2 mL
1 tsp	EACH: cinnamon, ginger	5 mL
1	egg	1
3/4 cup	skim milk	175 mL
1/2 cup	melted Country Crock Margarine	125 mL
1/4 cup	dark molasses	50 mL
	Rhubarb Sauce (recipe follows)	

In a large bowl, combine flour, sugar, baking soda, salt and spices. In a medium bowl, beat egg, milk, margarine and molasses until well blended. Pour liquid ingredients into dry ingredients; stir just until mixed. Spoon batter into a greased 8-inch (2 L) square pan. Bake at 350°F (180°C) 35–40 minutes. Serve with Rhubarb Sauce.

Microwave: Line bottom of pan with waxed paper. Prepare batter as above. Heat at MEDIUM (50%) 6 minutes; turn after 3 minutes. Heat at HIGH (100%) 2–3 minutes. Let stand 5–10 minutes directly on counter before removing from pan.

Makes 6 servings.

TIP: For a stronger ginger flavor, increase ginger to 1 1/2 tsp (7 mL).

Calories per serving: 307   Iron, vitamin A and thiamin: Good

RHUBARB SAUCE

Preparation: 5 minutes   Cook: about 20 minutes

4 cups	chopped fresh *or* frozen rhubarb	1 L
1/2 cup	sugar	125 mL
2 tbsp	Country Crock Margarine	25 mL

In a medium saucepan, combine all ingredients. Cover, cook slowly over medium heat about 20 minutes or until fruit is tender. Serve warm or cold over Gingerbread Cake.

Microwave: In a 6-cup (1.5 L) covered casserole, combine all ingredients. Heat at HIGH (100%) 6–7 minutes, stirring once. Let stand 5 minutes.

Makes approximately 1 1/2 cups (375 mL).

Calories per 1 tbsp (15 mL): 19   Low fat

VARIATION

Strawberry Sauce: Replace 2 cups (500 mL) rhubarb with 2 cups (500 mL) strawberries.

DOUBLE TREAT CHOCOLATE TORTE

Preparation: about 10 minutes   Cook: 35 minutes

This recipe proves that a low-calorie chocolate dessert can still be a chocoholic's dream.

1 cup	all-purpose flour	250 mL
1/3 cup	unsweetened cocoa	75 mL
1 tsp	Blue Ribbon Double Action Baking Powder	5 mL
1/2 cup	Becel Margarine	125 mL
2/3 cup	sugar	150 mL
1 tsp	vanilla	5 mL
3/4 cup	skim milk	175 mL
1	egg white	1
2 tbsp	icing sugar, sifted (optional)	25 mL
	Decadent Chocolate Sauce (recipe follows)	

Line a 9-inch (1.5 L) round cake pan with waxed paper; lightly grease paper. Dust with extra cocoa. In a medium bowl, combine flour, cocoa and baking powder. In another medium bowl, cream margarine, sugar and vanilla together until light and fluffy. Add dry ingredients to creamed mixture alternately with milk until combined. In a small bowl, beat egg white until stiff but not dry; fold into batter. Pour batter into pan. Bake at 350°F (180°C) 35 minutes. Cool cake in pan 5 minutes; invert onto rack; cool completely. Sprinkle with sifted icing sugar. Serve with Decadent Chocolate Sauce, if desired.

Microwave: Prepare batter and cake pan as above. Pour batter into pan. Cook at LOW (30%) 6 minutes (rotate pan after half the cooking time) and then at MEDIUM-HIGH (70%) 4–6 minutes or until toothpick inserted in center comes out clean. Let stand directly on counter top 5–10 minutes before removing from pan. Carefully peel off waxed paper, cool completely and sprinkle with icing sugar.

Makes 8 servings.

TIP: Add 1–2 tsp (5–10 mL) cinnamon to your favorite chocolate cake recipe or cake mix.

Calories per serving: 251, without Chocolate Sauce

DECADENT CHOCOLATE SAUCE   Preparation: about 5 minutes   Cook: about 2 minutes

While the table is being cleared between courses, you can make this quick chocolate sauce. Serve it over Double Treat Chocolate Torte, ice cream, angel cake or a pudding. It's also a chocolate lover's dream as a fondue dip for fresh fruit.

1/3 cup	sugar	75 mL
1/4 cup	unsweetened cocoa	50 mL
1 tbsp	cornstarch	15 mL
1 cup	water	250 mL
3 tbsp	Becel Margarine	45 mL
1 1/2 tsp	vanilla	7 mL

In a small saucepan, mix sugar, cocoa and cornstarch. Gradually add water, mixing until smooth. Cook over medium heat until mixture comes to a boil; simmer 1–2 minutes. Add margarine and vanilla; cool.

Microwave: In a 4-cup (1 L) measure, combine sauce ingredients. Heat at MEDIUM-HIGH (70%) 3–5 minutes or until thick; stir once or twice.

Makes 1 cup (250 mL) sauce.

Calories per 1 tbsp (15 mL): 41

VARIATIONS

Cinnamon Chocolate Sauce: Add 1/2 tsp (2 mL) cinnamon to Chocolate Sauce.

Mocha Sauce: Add 2 tsp (10 mL) instant coffee granules to hot Chocolate Sauce. Stir until dissolved.

STRAWBERRIES IN CHOCOLATE CUPS

Preparation: about 30 minutes   Chill: 30 minutes

When I taught cooking classes, this simple dessert recipe was one of the most popular with my students. If you have time, prepare the strawberry filling; if you don't, fill the chocolate cups with ice cream and top with fresh fruit; or fill with fresh fruit and Easy Dessert Glaze (page 126). The variations are endless. This dessert freezes well.

CHOCOLATE CUP SAUCE

3	squares semi-sweet chocolate	3
1 tbsp	hard margarine *or* butter	15 mL

In a small saucepan, melt chocolate and margarine; stir until smooth. Arrange 8–10 small foil muffin cups in a muffin pan. Spread or pour chocolate mixture evenly over bottom and sides by rotating muffin cup (or use back of spoon). Chill 30 minutes before filling with Strawberry Cream Filling.

STRAWBERRY CREAM FILLING

1	pouch Lucky Whip Dessert Topping Mix	1
¼ cup	milk	50 mL
¼ cup	orange liqueur	50 mL
2 cups	strawberries, divided	500 mL
	Mint leaves (optional)	

Prepare dessert topping mix according to package directions using milk and orange liqueur (omit vanilla). Fold in ¾ cup (175 mL) mashed berries. Place a strawberry half in bottom of each chilled chocolate cup. Spoon in cream filling and chill. Remove paper. Garnish with sliced strawberries and mint leaves, if desired.

Makes 8–10 servings.

Calories per chocolate cup: 127   Vitamin C: Excellent

LEMON CURD

Preparation: about 5 minutes   Cook: 25 minutes

With Lemon Curd in the refrigerator, last-minute desserts are a snap. Bake up some frozen tart shells and spoon in this tangy filling or spread it between layers of white or angel food cake.

6	eggs, slightly beaten	6
2	egg yolks, slightly beaten	2
2 cups	sugar	500 mL
¾ cup	lemon juice	175 mL
1 cup	Country Crock Margarine, softened	250 mL
¼ cup	grated lemon peel	50 mL

In top of a double boiler, combine all ingredients. Cook over low heat, stirring frequently, 25 minutes or until thickened. Remove from heat; let cool. Store, tightly covered, in refrigerator for up to 1 week. Use as a filling for small tart shells or layer cake.

Microwave: In an 8-cup (2 L) bowl, combine all ingredients. Heat at MEDIUM (50%) 10–12 minutes, stirring every 2–3 minutes, until thickened. Cool and store as above.

Makes approximately 4 cups (1 L).

Calories per ¼ cup (50 mL): 49

CELEBRATION FROSTING

Preparation: about 5 minutes   Cook: about 1 minute

The flavorings of this frosting can be varied to complement any type of cake you bake. Experiment! How about a chocolate cake iced with Luscious Cappucino? Or how about Creamy Fruit Melba with angel food? Or...?

1 tsp	Knox Unflavoured Gelatine	5 mL
1/4 cup	sugar*	50 mL
2 tbsp	cold water	25 mL
	Frosting Flavors (recipes follow)	
2	containers (250 mL) whipping cream	2
	or	
2	pouches Lucky Whip Dessert Topping Mix	2

*Reduce to 2 tbsp (25 mL) if using topping

Calories per 1 tbsp (15 mL): 49

In a small saucepan, mix gelatine with sugar; add cold water; cook and stir over low heat until gelatine is completely dissolved, about 1 minute. Add a Frosting Flavor. Remove from heat; cool completely. In a large bowl, beat cream until almost stiff; add gelatine mixture, beat until stiff. Or prepare dessert topping mix with milk according to pouch directions; beat in gelatine mixture.

Makes sufficient frosting for a 13 × 9-inch (3.5 L) pan or two 9-inch (1.5 L) layer pans.

FROSTING FLAVORS

Luscious Cappucino: Add 1 tbsp (15 mL) instant coffee granules and 1/2 tsp (2 mL) cinnamon to gelatine mixture. If desired, fold in 1/3 cup (75 mL) semi-sweet chocolate chips to beaten mixture. Use to frost a chocolate or mocha cake. Garnish with chocolate curls or fresh flowers.
Creamy Fruit Melba: Add 1 cup (250 mL) puréed fresh peaches or nectarines to cooled gelatine. Fold 1 cup (250 mL) fresh raspberries into beaten mixture. Use to frost a white, golden or angel food cake. Garnish with extra peach slices and raspberries, if desired.
Velvet Liqueur: Add 3 tbsp (45 mL) liqueur (e.g. crème de menthe, Triple Sec or coffee liqueur) to gelatine mixture. Use to frost an orange or chocolate cake. Garnish, if desired, with chocolate curls.

DESSERT FRUIT TACOS

Preparation: about 10 minutes

This is another winning dessert from your shortcut shelf. Taco shells, dusted with sugar and cinnamon and filled with fresh fruit, can be prepared in separate stages and assembled at the last minute.

3 cups	prepared, fresh or canned fruit*, drained	750 mL
1/4 cup	coconut	50 mL
1/2 cup	dairy sour cream	125 mL
1	package MexiCasa Taco Shells (10)	1
1/4 cup	icing sugar	50 mL
1/2 tsp	cinnamon *or* nutmeg	2 mL

* Use a combination of any of the following fruits: melon balls (e.g. watermelon, cantaloupe, honeydew), strawberries, raspberries, green or red seedless grapes, pineapple chunks, orange sections, sliced bananas or kiwi.

Combine drained fruit, coconut and sour cream; chill. Heat taco shells according to package directions. In a plastic bag, combine icing sugar and cinnamon. Shake warm shells in this mixture until lightly coated. Fill each shell with 1/3 cup (75 mL) fruit mixture; sprinkle with extra coconut or cinnamon.

Makes 10 tacos.

Calories per taco: 148

CALORIE-REDUCED FROSTING

Preparation: about 10 minutes   Cook: about 3 minutes

There's an old adage that says you can't have your cake and eat it too. However, this calorie-reduced frosting makes it possible — in many flavors.

2 tbsp	all-purpose flour	25 mL
½ cup	EACH: skim milk, Country Crock Margarine, icing sugar	125 mL
1 tsp	vanilla	5 mL

In a small saucepan, combine flour and milk. Cook and stir, about 3 minutes, until smooth and thickened; set aside to cool. In a small bowl, cream together margarine and icing sugar. Add cooked mixture and vanilla; beat until light and fluffy.

Makes sufficient frosting to frost 1 layer cake or 1 small angel food cake.

Calories per 1 tbsp (15 mL): 49

VARIATIONS

Chocolate Frosting: Add 2 tbsp (25 mL) cocoa.
Mocha Frosting: Add 1 tbsp (15 mL) cocoa and ½ tsp (2 mL) instant coffee granules.
Coffee Frosting: Add 1 tsp (5 mL) instant coffee granules.

Orange or Lemon Frosting: Replace vanilla with ½ tsp (2 mL) orange or lemon peel.

TIP: Frostings made with icing sugar stay moist longer if you add a pinch of baking powder. It prevents hardening and cracking.

ORANGE BLOSSOM BUNDT CAKE

Preparation: about 10 minutes   Cook: about 45 minutes

If you want to use this cake for a special occasion, decorate it with a glaze. Then choose flowers in rainbow colors and tuck them into the center of the cake and around the edges. Instant decorating!

1 cup	Becel Margarine	250 mL
1½ cups	sugar	375 mL
1½ tsp	grated orange peel	7 mL
1 tsp	vanilla	5 mL
2¾ cups	all-purpose flour	675 mL
½ tsp	EACH: baking soda, cinnamon	2 mL
¼ tsp	EACH: nutmeg, ginger	1 mL
⅛ tsp	ground cloves	0.5 mL
4	egg whites	4
1¼ cups	buttermilk	300 mL
1 tbsp	icing sugar	15 mL
	or	
	Orange Glaze (recipe follows)	

In a large mixing bowl, cream margarine and sugar until light and fluffy. Beat in orange peel and vanilla. Sift together flour, baking soda, cinnamon, nutmeg, ginger and cloves. Beat egg whites until stiff peaks form. Add dry ingredients alternately with buttermilk to margarine mixture. Mix just until dry ingredients are moistened. Fold egg whites into batter. Turn batter into a greased 12-cup (3 L) bundt pan. Bake at 350°F (180°C) 45–50 minutes or until cake tester inserted in center comes out clean. Cool in pan on wire rack 15 minutes. Remove from pan and cool completely. Sprinkle with icing sugar or drizzle with Orange Glaze just before serving.

Makes 16–18 servings.

ORANGE GLAZE

Preparation: about 5 minutes

3 tbsp	fresh orange juice	45 mL
½ tsp	grated orange peel	2 mL
1 cup	icing sugar, sifted	250 mL

In a small bowl, stir together orange juice, peel and sugar until smooth.

Calories per serving: 274

ORANGE LIQUEUR SAUCE

Preparation: about 3 minutes   Cook: about 5 minutes

You can make an instant gourmet dessert by filling scooped-out orange halves with ice cream topped with orange liqueur sauce. Garnish with orange sections and mint leaves.

2 tbsp	Becel Margarine	25 mL
2 tbsp	sugar	25 mL
1 tbsp	cornstarch	15 mL
¼ cup	water	50 mL
	Grated peel of 1 orange	
½ cup	orange juice	125 mL
1–2 tbsp	orange liqueur	15–25 mL

In a small saucepan, over low heat, melt margarine. Add sugar, cornstarch, water and orange peel. Cook over low heat, stirring until smooth and thickened, about 5 minutes. Add orange juice and liqueur; cook, stirring constantly until heated through.

Microwave: In a small bowl, melt margarine at HIGH (100%) 15 seconds. Add sugar, cornstarch, water and orange peel. Heat at HIGH 2–3 minutes; stir several times.

Makes approximately 1 cup (250 mL).

Calories per 1 tbsp (15 mL): 24   Low fat

VARIATIONS

Kahlua Sauce: Omit orange peel. Replace orange juice with coffee and orange liqueur with Kahlua.

Drambuie Sauce: Replace orange liqueur with Drambuie.

Cherry Brandy Sauce: Replace orange juice with water and orange liqueur with Cherry Brandy.

Amaretto Sauce: Omit orange peel. Replace orange juice with water and 1 tsp (5 mL) almond extract, and orange liqueur with Amaretto.

UNBAKED CHOCOLATE MARBLE CHEESECAKE

Preparation: about 15 minutes   Cook: 4 minutes   Chill: about 1 hour

The tempting tastes of chocolate and cheesecake are combined for this luscious dessert. The cinnamon adds a scented spiciness.

1½ cups	chocolate wafer crumbs	375 mL
½ tsp	cinnamon	2 mL
⅓ cup	margarine *or* butter, melted	75 mL
1	pouch Knox Unflavoured Gelatine	1
¾ cup	sugar	175 mL
½ cup	milk	125 mL
2	eggs	2
1	package (250 g) cream cheese, softened	1
1 tsp	vanilla	5 mL
2 tsp	grated orange peel	10 mL
2 tbsp	orange liqueur (optional)	25 mL
1 cup	dairy sour cream	250 mL
6	squares semi-sweet chocolate, melted and cooled	6

In a small bowl, combine crumbs, cinnamon and margarine; press mixture into bottom of 9-inch (23 cm) springform pan. In a medium saucepan, mix gelatine with sugar; add milk and eggs. Cook and stir over low heat for 4 minutes until gelatine is completely dissolved and mixture is slightly thickened; cool. Combine cream cheese, vanilla, orange peel or liqueur; beat until smooth and creamy. Blend in sour cream. Pour three-quarters of this mixture into springform pan. Add melted chocolate to remaining cream cheese mixture; blend well. Drop chocolate mixture in spoonfuls over cream mixture in pan. Carefully run a knife through the batter to create a marble effect. Refrigerate until firm, about 1 hour. To serve, loosen around side of pan with a sharp knife, release springform and remove side of pan.

Makes 12–16 servings.

Calories per serving: 294

BLUEBERRY VELVET CHEESECAKE

Preparation: about 15 minutes   Chill: about 2 hours

Swirling blueberry filling through this velvety cheesecake and adding almonds to the crust makes an exceptional dessert.

2	pouches Knox Unflavoured Gelatine	2
¾ cup	sugar, divided	175 mL
1 cup	boiling water	250 mL
2	packages (250 g) cream cheese, softened	2
1 cup	cottage cheese	250 mL
1	container (250 mL) whipping cream	1
1 tbsp	vanilla	15 mL
2 tsp	grated lemon peel	10 mL
1	Graham Cracker Almond Crust (recipe follows)	1
1	can (19 oz/540 mL) blueberry pie filling	1

In a small bowl, combine gelatine with ½ cup (125 mL) sugar. Add boiling water; stir constantly until gelatine is completely dissolved. In a medium bowl, beat cream cheese and cottage cheese; add whipping cream and continue beating until smooth. Slowly beat in dissolved gelatine, remaining sugar, vanilla and lemon peel. Pour mixture into prepared crust. As cream cheese mixture begins to set, place spoonfuls of blueberry filling in a circle, 1 inch (2.5 cm) from outer edge of cheese cake. To create swirl pattern, draw a knife through the blueberry filling towards the center of the cake, cutting into the cheese filling in a figure eight pattern. Leave an unswirled 2-inch (5 cm) diameter circle in the center of the cake. Chill until set. To serve, loosen around side of pan with a sharp knife, release springform and remove side of pan.

Makes 12–16 servings.

GRAHAM CRACKER ALMOND CRUST

1 cup	graham cracker crumbs	250 mL
½ cup	ground almonds	125 mL
2 tbsp	sugar	25 mL
¼ cup	margarine *or* butter, melted	50 mL
½ tsp	almond extract	2 mL

In a small bowl, combine all ingredients. Press into bottom and sides of 9-inch (23 cm) springform pan; chill.

Calories per serving: 340

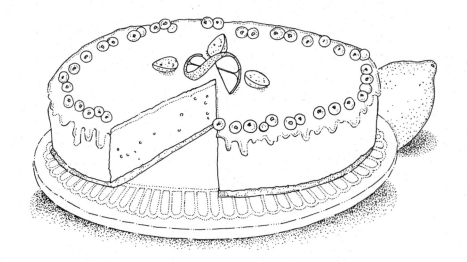

INDULGENCES

When it's too hot to bake, indulge yourself with one of these chilled pies and get a head start on your meal preparation. Save on calories as well.

CHOCOLATE INDULGENCE   Preparation: about 30 minutes   Chill: about 2 hours

¾ cup	sugar, divided	175 mL
⅔ cup	cocoa	150 mL
2	pouches Knox Unflavoured Gelatine	2
1 cup	water	250 mL
3 tbsp	Becel Margarine	45 mL
2 cups	low-fat cottage cheese	500 mL
3	egg whites	3
1	Graham Cracker Crust (recipe follows)	1

In a medium saucepan, combine ½ cup (125 mL) sugar, cocoa and gelatine with water. Cook over medium heat 3–4 minutes; stir in margarine. Cool. In a blender or food processor, blend cottage cheese until creamy; add cooled chocolate mixture. In a medium bowl, beat egg whites until foamy, add remaining sugar, beat until stiff peaks form. Fold egg whites into cooled mixture. Chill to thicken mixture, about 20 minutes; turn into prepared crust; chill until firm, about 2 hours.

Makes 6 servings.

Calories per serving: 348

CREAMY CHEESE INDULGENCE   Preparation: about 8 minutes   Chill: about 2 hours

1	pouch Knox Unflavoured Gelatine	1
2 tbsp	EACH: cold water, lemon juice	25 mL
½ cup	skim milk, scalded	125 mL
2	egg whites	2
½ cup	icing sugar	125 mL
2 cups	low-fat cottage cheese	500 mL
1 tsp	grated lemon peel	5 mL
1	Graham Cracker Crust (recipe follows)	1

In a blender or food processor, sprinkle gelatine over cold water and lemon juice. Let stand 3–4 minutes. Add hot milk, process at low speed until gelatine is completely dissolved. Add remaining ingredients; blend at high speed until smooth. Pour into prepared crust; chill until firm, about 2 hours.

Makes 6 servings.

Calories per serving: 217   Low fat

GRAHAM CRACKER CRUST   Preparation: about 5 minutes   Cook: 5 minutes

1¼ cups	graham or vanilla wafer crumbs	300 mL
2 tbsp	Becel Margarine, melted	25 mL
1 tsp	cinnamon (optional)	5 mL

Combine crumbs, margarine and cinnamon. Press into a 9-inch (23 cm) pie plate. Bake at 375°F (190°C) 5 minutes. Cool.

Microwave: In a 9-inch (23 cm) glass pie plate, melt margarine at HIGH (100%) 30 seconds. Mix in crumbs and cinnamon. Press mixture firmly against bottom and sides of plate. Heat at HIGH (100%) 1½–2 minutes; rotate plate once during cooking. Cool.

VARIATIONS

Fresh Fruit Indulgence: Top with your choice of fruit just before serving.

White Christmas Indulgence: Top with grated coconut and halved red and green cherries.

EASY ELEGANT BAVARIAN PIE

Preparation: about 10 minutes   Chill: about 2 hours

It's always an advantage to have a recipe for an elegant dessert you can make in minutes with staples from your freezer and cupboard. And this is it!

2	pouches Knox Unflavoured Gelatine	2
1¼ cups	ginger ale, white wine *or* champagne, divided	300 mL
1	container (250 mL) whipping cream, heated to boiling *or*	1
2	pouches Lucky Whip Dessert Topping Mix *and*	2
1 cup	milk	250 mL
1 cup	frozen raspberry, strawberry *or* orange juice concentrate, thawed	250 mL
½ cup	water	125 mL

1	Macaroon Crumb Crust (recipe follows) *or*	1
1	Graham Cracker Almond Crust (page 133)	1

In a blender, sprinkle gelatine over ¼ cup (50 mL) ginger ale. Let stand 3–4 minutes. Add hot cream, process at low speed about 2 minutes until gelatine is completely dissolved, or add dessert topping mix to blender, heat 1 cup (250 mL) milk to boiling, pour over gelatine in blender and proceed as above. Add remaining ginger ale, fruit juice concentrate and water; blend at high speed until smooth. Pour into prepared crust; chill until firm, about 2 hours.

Makes approximately 8 servings.

MACAROON CRUMB CRUST

Crumble 10–12 macaroon cookies (about 2 cups/ 500 mL crumbs). Press into a deep 9-inch (23 cm) pie plate. Bake at 350°F (180°C) 8 minutes; cool.

Calories per serving: 309   Fiber: Good

BRULÉE SABAYON

Preparation: about 15 minutes   Broil: about 5 minutes

This magnificent showpiece recipe can be made almost totally from your shortcut shelf.

1	package (92 g) vanilla pudding and pie filling	1
1 cup	milk	250 mL
1	pouch Lucky Whip Dessert Topping Mix	1
¼ cup	EACH: milk and brandy, sherry *or* rum *or*	50 mL
½ cup	milk *and*	125 mL
2 tsp	vanilla extract	10 mL
½ cup	brown sugar, packed	125 mL
½ cup	slivered almonds Seasonal fresh fruit	125 mL

In a medium saucepan, cook pudding and pie filling with 1 cup (250 mL) milk according to package directions. Cover surface of pudding with plastic wrap and cool to room temperature. Whip dessert topping mix with milk and liquor, or with ½ cup (125 mL) milk and vanilla according to package directions. Fold into cooled pudding. Pour into a large ovenproof shallow baking dish. Sprinkle with brown sugar and almonds. Place 3 inches (7 cm) under a preheated broiler until sugar melts and starts to brown, about 5 minutes. Watch closely to prevent sugar burning. Serve warm or cold with prepared fruit.

Makes 5–6 servings.

Calories per serving: 308, without fruit   Calcium: Good

PUMPKIN CRUNCH PIE

Preparation: about 15 minutes   Chill: about 1 hour

Canned pumpkin from your shortcut shelf can be turned into a sensational year-round dessert. This pie is a pleasing contrast of smooth and crunchy textures. Also included in the recipe is a hurry-up method for setting gelatine.

1¼ cups	graham cracker crumbs	300 mL
¼ cup	sugar	50 mL
½ cup	finely chopped pecans	125 mL
⅓ cup	margarine *or* butter, melted	75 mL
2	pouches Knox Unflavoured Gelatine	2
½ cup	cold milk	125 mL
½ cup	scalded milk	125 mL
¾ cup	firmly packed brown sugar	175 mL
1 tsp	cinnamon	5 mL
½ tsp	EACH: salt and nutmeg	2 mL
¼ tsp	ginger	1 mL
1 cup	light cream	250 mL
1	can (14 oz/398 mL) pumpkin	1
6	ice cubes	6

In a small bowl, combine crumbs, sugar, pecans and margarine. Reserve ¼ cup (50 mL) mixture for garnish; press remainder into a deep 9-inch (23 cm) pie plate. Bake at 375°F (190°C) 5 minutes. Cool. In a blender, sprinkle gelatine over cold milk; let stand 1 minute. Add scalded milk; process at low speed about 2 minutes until gelatine is completely dissolved. Add brown sugar, cinnamon, salt, nutmeg, ginger and cream; cover and process at high speed about 1 minute. Add pumpkin, process at high speed about 30 seconds. Remove center top cover and, with blender still running, add ice cubes one at a time. Process at high speed until ice is melted. Chill to thicken mixture, about 10 minutes; turn into prepared pie shell. Sprinkle with reserved crumb mixture. Chill until set, about 1 hour.

Makes 8 servings.

Calories per serving: 352   Vitamin A: Excellent   Iron: Good

CINNAMON APPLE TART

Preparation: about 15 minutes   Cook: about 45 minutes

There's nothing like the heavenly smell of baking apples and cinnamon wafting through the house. This simply prepared dessert is a warm treat on cold winter days.

⅓ cup	EACH: brown sugar, Monarch Cinnamon Spread	75 mL
1 tbsp	lemon juice	15 mL
3	apples, peeled, cored and sliced	3
	Raisins *or* pecans (optional)	
¼ cup	Monarch Cinnamon Spread	50 mL
2 tbsp	sugar	25 mL
1	egg	1
⅓ cup	molasses	75 mL
¾ cup	all-purpose flour	175 mL
1 tsp	Blue Ribbon Double Action Baking Powder	5 mL
½ tsp	EACH: baking soda, ginger, salt	2 mL
⅓ cup	boiling water	75 mL

In an 8-inch (2 L) square or round pan, combine brown sugar, cinnamon spread and lemon juice. Bake at 350°F (180°C) 2–3 minutes, remove and spread to cover bottom of pan. Arrange apple slices on top of mixture. Sprinkle raisins or pecans over apples, if desired. In a small bowl, cream ¼ cup (50 mL) cinnamon spread, sugar, egg and molasses. In another bowl, combine dry ingredients; add to creamed mixture. Stir in boiling water. Spread batter over apples. Bake at 350°F (180°C) 40–45 minutes. Cool 5 minutes, remove from pan and serve warm.

Makes 6 servings.

Calories per serving: 166

GRANDMA'S BAKED APPLES

Preparation: about 15 minutes   Cook: about 1½ hours

This always brings back comforting memories of childhood visits to my grandparents' home. Grandma knew this was my favorite dessert and always had it ready and waiting for me.

4	tart baking apples	4
½ cup	raisins *or* currants	125 mL
2 tbsp	chopped dates	25 mL
½ tsp	cinnamon	2 mL
2 tbsp	Country Crock Margarine, divided	25 mL
1½ cups	unsweetened apple juice, divided	375 mL
1½ tsp	cornstarch	7 mL
4	packets low-calorie sugar substitute (e.g. Equal)	4

Core apples. In a small bowl, combine raisins, dates, cinnamon and 1 tbsp (15 mL) margarine. Stuff apples with mixture and top each with remaining margarine. Reserve any remaining raisin mixture to add to sauce. Place apples in a shallow baking pan. Pour 1 cup (250 mL) apple juice over apples. Bake at 275°F (140°C) 1½–2 hours. Remove apples; reserve juice. In a small saucepan, blend cornstarch with remaining apple juice and cooked apple juice; add any reserved raisin mixture. Cook until thickened, 2–3 minutes; add sugar substitute. Pour sauce over apples. Serve warm.

Microwave: Core apples; peel a strip of skin around top of apple to allow steam to escape. Stuff apples as above; place in pan, pour apple juice into pan. Cover with plastic wrap. Heat at HIGH (100%) 6–7 minutes; spoon sauce over at 3 minutes and rotate dish. Let stand 2–3 minutes.

Makes 4 servings.

Calories per apple: 226   Fiber and vitamin C: Excellent

ECSTASY

Preparation: about 15 minutes   Cook: 15 minutes   Chill: overnight

This is one of those recipes that is turning up everywhere. The American version is Mississippi Mud Pie; the Canadian version, Mud Pie. However, Ecstasy more accurately sums up the reaction to this quickly made dessert. Be sure to try it!

1 cup	EACH: chopped pecans, all-purpose flour	250 mL
½ cup	Imperial Margarine	125 mL
3 tbsp	sugar	45 mL
2	pouches Lucky Whip Dessert Topping Mix	2
1 cup	milk, divided	250 mL
1 tsp	vanilla, divided	5 mL
1	package (250 g) cream cheese, softened	1
1 cup	icing sugar	250 mL
2 cups	milk	500 mL
1	package (113 g) EACH: instant chocolate, instant vanilla pudding	1
	Shaved chocolate	

In a medium bowl, combine pecans, flour, margarine and sugar. Press into a 13 × 9-inch (3.5 L) pan. Bake at 350°F (180°C) 15 minutes. Cool. Prepare 1 pouch dessert topping mix according to package directions with ½ cup (125 mL) milk and ½ tsp (2 mL) vanilla; mix with cream cheese and icing sugar. Spread over cooked base. In a medium bowl, beat 2 cups (500 mL) milk and chocolate and vanilla puddings. Spread evenly over cream layer. Prepare second pouch of dessert topping mix with remaining milk and vanilla; spread over pudding layer. Sprinkle with shaved chocolate. Refrigerate overnight before serving.

Makes 10–12 servings.

TIPS: 1. This recipe may be prepared in two 8-inch (2 L) square pans — freeze one for later use. You may wish to double the crust ingredients. 2. For a change of pace, replace chocolate pudding with pistachio or butterscotch.

Calories per serving: 393   Vitamin A: Good

KNOX ICE CREAM

Preparation: about 40 minutes   Freeze: 1–1½ hours

When you make ice cream with Knox Gelatine, it will have a smoother texture and ice crystals will not develop. After you've made the recipe base, choose from the ice cream parlor selection of flavors given below.

1	pouch Knox Unflavoured Gelatine	1
3/4 cup	sugar	175 mL
2 cups	milk	500 mL
2 tsp	vanilla extract	10 mL
2	containers (250 mL) whipping cream	2

In a medium saucepan, mix gelatine and sugar; add milk. Cook and stir over low heat until gelatine is completely dissolved, about 3 minutes. Stir in vanilla. Chill, stirring occasionally, until mixture mounds slightly when dropped from a spoon. Whip cream until almost stiff; fold into gelatine mixture. Pour into a 13 × 9-inch (3.5 L) pan; freeze, stirring the mixture once or twice during freezing. Let stand 5–10 minutes before serving.

Makes 6–8 servings.

Calories per serving: 316   Vitamin A: Good

VARIATIONS

Cherry Vanilla Ice Cream: Stir ½ cup (125 mL) chopped maraschino cherries into the partially frozen ice cream. Freeze until firm.

Chocolate Candy Bar Ice Cream: Stir one coarsely crushed chocolate candy bar into the partially frozen ice cream. Freeze until firm.

Fruit Ice Cream: Reduce sugar to ½ cup (125 mL), milk to 1 cup (250 mL) and stir 1 thawed package (425 g) frozen sweetened fruit into the partially frozen ice cream. Freeze until firm.

Butterscotch Pecan Ice Cream: Stir ¼ cup (50 mL) coarsely chopped, toasted pecans and ½ cup (125 mL) butterscotch syrup into the partially frozen ice cream. Freeze until firm.

Liqueur Ice Cream: Replace vanilla with 2 tbsp (25 mL) liqueur (e.g. Grand Marnier, crème de menthe, crème de cacao).

Chocolate Chip Ice Cream: Replace vanilla with ½ tsp (2 mL) peppermint *or* 2 tbsp (25 mL) Kahlua. Stir ½ cup (125 mL) chocolate chips into partially frozen ice cream.

LOW-CALORIE FROZEN FRUIT YOGURT

Preparation: about 5 minutes   Freeze: 3 hours

Sometimes, you have "a bit of this and not much of that" when you look at the fruits in your refrigerator. Mash them together to make this luscious, low-calorie dessert with a cool, tangy taste.

1	pouch Knox Unflavoured Gelatine	1
¼ cup	orange juice	50 mL
1 cup	2 percent milk, heated	250 mL
2 cups	low-fat plain yogurt	500 mL
8	packets low-calorie sugar substitute (e.g. Equal)	8
2	medium bananas *or* kiwi, mashed	2
	or	
1½ cups	mashed fruit (e.g. peaches, strawberries, raspberries or blueberries)	375 mL

In a small bowl, sprinkle gelatine over orange juice; let stand 1 minute. Add hot milk; stir constantly until gelatine is completely dissolved. Cool slightly. Add yogurt, sugar substitute and prepared fruit. Freeze in an 8-inch (2L) square pan, stirring 2–3 times during freezing. Let stand 15–20 minutes before serving.

Makes 5–6 servings.

Calories per serving: 122   Calcium and vitamin C: Good

ICE CREAM TACOS

Preparation: about 5 minutes

Making their own sundaes is a popular birthday treat for my children. These Ice Cream Tacos are a more sophisticated version of the same idea. Adults like them too!

1	package MexiCasa Taco Shells (10)	1
¼ cup	icing sugar	50 mL
1 tsp	cocoa	5 mL
4 cups	vanilla ice cream	1 L

Toppings: chocolate or caramel sauce, chopped peanuts, cherries, chocolate chips or grated chocolate, coconut, finely diced fruit (e.g. bananas, apples, strawberries).

Calories per taco: 189, without toppings

Heat taco shells according to package directions. In a plastic bag, combine icing sugar and cocoa. Shake warm shells in this mixture until lightly coated. Partially fill shells with ice cream; top with sundae sauce and your choice of toppings. Serve immediately or freeze until serving time.

Makes 10 ice cream tacos.

VARIATION

Chocolate Ice Cream Tacos: Melt 1½ cups (375 mL) chocolate chips. Dip the edges of taco shells into melted chocolate. Refrigerate shells to set chocolate.

TIPS: 1. Use ice cream you can slice for easier filling of taco shells. 2. After scooping or slicing ice cream from the container, press a piece of plastic wrap against the surface of the remaining ice cream, close the container and return to the freezer. Next time you won't be greeted by unwanted ice crystals on the surface.

HERBAL SORBET

Preparation: about 10 minutes   Freeze: about 2 hours

Sorbet is even more refreshing when you use herbal tea with its subtle citrus tang. It can be used either for a light dessert or as a palate cleanser at a gourmet dinner.

6	Lipton Herbal Tea Bags	6
2 cups	boiling water	500 mL
¼ cup	liquid honey	50 mL
	or	
½ cup	sugar	125 mL
	Mint leaves (optional)	

In a medium saucepan, pour boiling water over tea bags. Brew 5 minutes; remove tea bags. Stir in honey, heat until melted. Cool. Place in a shallow pan; cover, freeze until almost solid, about 1 hour. In a blender or food processor, beat sherbet until smooth and creamy; return to freezer, freeze until mushy, about 1 hour. Serve scoops of sherbet in stemmed glasses garnished with mint leaves, if desired.

Makes 5–6 servings.

TIP: Lemon Soother, Citrus Sunset, Tangy or Gentle Orange are appropriate herbal teas.

Calories per serving: 36   Low fat

VARIATION

Fruit Sorbet: To cool syrup, add 2 cups (500 mL) mashed strawberries, peaches *or* raspberries.

BEVERAGES AND SANDWICHES

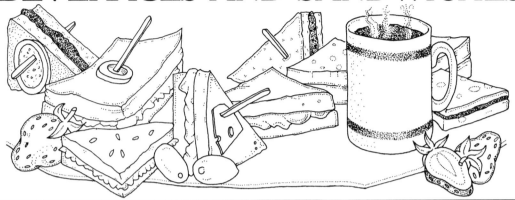

AFTERNOON TEA

The lovely custom of Afternoon Tea is making a comeback. It is being served in exclusive hotels, in fine restaurants and in many homes. Why not discover this easy and elegant way of entertaining for yourself? It is a way to relax from the hectic demands of today's lifestyles.

Although you need serve only two or three types of sandwiches and a selection of sweets with tea, planning and presentation are important. Choose fresh flowers for the house. Arrange and garnish the food on attractive serving plates and use your best china, silverware and linens. Then, sit back, relax, and enjoy your friends.

The tradition of Afternoon Tea dates back to English Royalty. However, historians cannot decide whether it was Queen Catherine, wife of Charles II, or Ana, wife of the Seventh Duke of Bedford, who initiated the custom. Obviously, both ladies knew a good and easy way to entertain.

Afternoon Tea, which is also called Low Tea, is often served from 3:00–5:00 P.M. High Tea, served from 5:00–6:00 P.M., generally replaces supper in British rural areas. Heartier food is served, such as savoury meat pies, hearty sandwiches and egg dishes.

FORMAL TEA

A Formal Tea is given for a large group of people and is a stand-up affair. While the tea table was traditionally set with white linens, pastel linens are used today. Coordinate them with your floral centerpiece and china for an attractive table setting. You'll need a tea pot, tea cups and saucers, teaspoons, a sliced lemon tray, sugar bowl, milk pitcher and serviettes. Serve finger foods such as miniature sandwiches and sweets and, perhaps, salted nuts. To save time in serving tea to a large group, use a Tea Concentrate (page 143).

INFORMAL TEA

For an Informal Tea, a smaller group of people, who are seated, are served in the living room from a small table or tea wagon. It is set with the same items used for a Formal Tea, but food is served that requires a tea plate and cutlery. For superb tea, use the directions given for Hot Pot Tea (page 144).

TEA TYPES

Black tea, oolong tea and green tea all come from the same tea plant, but it is the processing of the leaf that determines the three basic types of tea. Altogether, there are 3,000 varieties of tea produced around the world, and they take their names from the areas in which they grow.

TEA ACCOMPANIMENTS

The traditional accompaniments for tea are lemon slices, milk and sugar. However, you can add some thin slices of orange or lime, sticks of cinnamon or whole cloves. Sometimes pastel-colored rock candy crystals, available in the specialty sections of large grocery stores, are used. You could also serve a selection of jams for a Russian style of tea-drinking. Place a spoonful of jam and a slice of lemon in the bottom of a teacup before pouring tea over it. Or perhaps you might like to serve an Herbal Tea such as Lemon Soother or Cinnamon Apple. All Lipton Herbal Teas are caffeine-free. Just be sure to pick a flavor to blend with your food.

HISTORY OF TEA

There are many legends about the origins of tea. It is said that Emperor Shen-Nung discovered tea in 2737 B.C. when leaves from a nearby tea plant dropped into his pot of boiling water. However, it wasn't until 1716 that the first shipment of tea reached Canada. Today tea is the most popular beverage in Canada and the rest of the world. Canadians alone drink over 11 billion cups a year. Next to water, tea is the most popular and least expensive beverage in the world.

In the tea trade, Sir Thomas Lipton was a great innovator and imaginative merchandiser. He was the first to package tea in quarter, half and one-pound packages. Professional tea tasters still maintain the quality of tea for which Lipton and Red Rose have become famous. The Red Rose name has represented the finest quality tea since 1894. The current Red Rose symbol—a long-stemmed rose—was adopted in 1957. When you want the perfect cup of tea, make sure you use Red Rose.

There's a great deal of history and romance in one small cup of clear, refreshing liquid.

TEA-TIME SANDWICHES

Trim crusts from assorted thinly sliced breads; cut into circles, rectangles, squares or triangles. Spread with Suggested Toppings (recipes follow). These sandwiches can be made in advance and frozen.

SUGGESTED TOPPINGS

Strawberry Cheese: Blend 1 package (250 g) cream cheese, softened with ¼ cup (50 mL) strawberry preserves; stir in 3 tbsp (45 mL) chopped pecans. Spread on date nut bread and garnish with pecan halves.

Dilled Shrimp: Combine 1 cup (250 mL) finely chopped cooked shrimp, ¼ cup (50 mL) sour cream, ½ teaspoon (2 mL) dill weed and salt and pepper to taste. Spread on brown or whole wheat bread and garnish with additional fresh dill.

Chicken Curry: Combine 1¾ cups (425 mL) finely chopped cooked chicken, ¼ cup (50 mL) each: mayonnaise and plain yogurt, ½ teaspoon (2 mL) curry powder and salt and pepper to taste. Spread on cinnamon raisin bread and garnish with sliced almonds.

PERKY PINWHEEL SANDWICHES

Preparation: about 45 minutes   Chill: several hours

When I was a child and tea was served at home, I always hoped the peanut butter and banana pinwheels would be left over. To that end, I carefully gauged each guest's selection of sandwiches. Nowadays, I wouldn't be as concerned — providing these delicious and sophisticated pinwheel sandwiches were offered for tea.

2	loaves, white or pumpernickel bread, sliced lengthwise (16 slices)	2
2 cups	Lipton Classic Onion Dip (page 10)	500 mL
	Festive Fillings (recipes follow)	

Trim crust from bread; flatten bread with a rolling pin. Choose two fillings. Spread each filling mixture evenly on 8 slices of bread; roll up. Wrap in waxed paper or plastic wrap and chill several hours. To serve, cut into thin slices.

Makes approximately 10 dozen sandwiches.

FESTIVE FILLINGS

Blue Cheese Walnut Filling: Combine 1 cup (250 mL) Lipton Onion Dip, 2 tbsp (25 mL) crumbled blue cheese and ½ cup (125 mL) finely chopped walnuts.

Fruity Curry Filling: Combine 1 cup (250 mL) Lipton Onion Dip, ¾ tsp (3 mL) curry powder, ½ cup (125 mL) chopped raisins, ½ cup (125 mL) finely chopped apple and 1 tbsp (15 mL) milk.

Wine, Cheese and Olive Filling: Combine 1 cup (250 mL) Lipton Onion Dip, ¾ cup (175 mL) grated Cheddar cheese and 2 tbsp (25 mL) red wine. Place 3 ripe, pitted olives across one end of each prepared slice; roll up starting at olive end.

TIPS: 1. If you don't have a straight eye for slicing, many bakeries will cut the bread for you. 2. These fillings do not freeze well.

TEA CONCENTRATES FOR A CROWD

If you're planning a large party where you'll be serving tea, try using these convenient concentrate methods for hot and iced tea. Simply follow these four steps and refer to the chart below for quantities.

CONCENTRATE METHODS FOR HOT AND ICED TEA
1. Bring fresh cold water to a full rolling boil and pour over tea bags or loose tea.
2. Cover and brew 5 minutes.
3. Remove tea bags, squeezing gently or strain loose tea. Keep at room temperature; do not refrigerate. (Use concentrate within 2 hours.)
4. For each cup of hot tea use 2 tbsp (25 mL) tea concentrate (use more or less according to strength desired). Fill with hot water. Serve with milk, sugar or lemon. For each glass of iced tea use 4 tbsp (50 mL) tea concentrate; fill with cold water. Serve with ice, sugar, lemon or mint.

CONCENTRATE PROPORTIONS

| | 25 servings | | 50 servings | | | 25 servings | | 50 servings | |
	Hot	Iced	Hot	Iced		Hot	Iced	Hot	Iced
Boiling Water	4 cups (1 L)	8 cups (2 L)	8 cups (2 L)	20 cups (5 L)					
Red Rose or PG Tips Tea Bags	13	20	25	40	Loose Tea	½ cup (125 mL)	1 cup (250 mL)	1 cup (250 mL)	2 cups (500 mL)

HOT POT TEA

1. Use freshly drawn cold water. Cold water is aerated (full of oxygen) and brings out the full character of tea.
2. Bring the water to a full, rolling boil. Boiling water releases the full flavor and fragrance from the tea leaves. Avoid boiling the water too long or boiling twice.
3. Temperature is very important for properly brewing tea. Fill the teapot with very hot water and let it stand for a few minutes to preheat.
4. Use one tea bag or teaspoon of loose tea per cup. This gives each cup the maximum flavor, color and body.
5. Pour in boiling water, cover and brew 3 to 5 minutes. Brewing longer than 5 minutes simply produces bitterness.
6. Squeeze the tea bag gently. If using loose tea, strain or remove the infuser. Serve, if desired, with sugar, honey or lemon.

TIP: Don't throw away leftover tea. Use it to water your plants. It's a terrific fertilizer!

SUPER ICED TEA

Next to water, no drink is more refreshing than iced tea. Easy to make perfectly every time, it is delicious plain or flavored. The traditional method of making iced tea begins with double strength hot tea. Use twice the amount of tea (either bags or loose tea) you would normally use for Hot Pot Tea.

OVERNIGHT ICED TEA

Fill a 4-cup (1 L) jar or pitcher with cold tap water. Add 8–10 tea bags. Cover. Place in the refrigerator at least 6 hours or overnight. Remove tea bags, squeezing against side of pitcher. Pour into ice-filled glasses. Garnish and sweeten to individual taste.

MULLED TEA PUNCH

Preparation: about 10 minutes

Ottawa relatives serve this punch after skating parties on the canal. Add orange slices, studded with cloves, to its steaming goodness.

4 cups	boiling water	1 L
6	Red Rose Tea Bags	6
5 cups	cranberry juice cocktail	1.25 L
1 cup	brown sugar	250 mL
6	whole cloves	6
6	whole allspice	6
1	cinnamon stick, broken	1
1	bottle (750 mL) Burgundy wine	1

In a saucepan, pour boiling water over tea bags; brew 5 minutes. Remove tea bags. Add cranberry juice, brown sugar and spices. Bring to a boil, then simmer, stirring occasionally, 5 minutes. Remove spices; stir in wine and heat through.

Makes approximately twenty ½-cup (125 mL) servings.

TIP: When making tea for a punch, brew it in a covered saucepan rather than a teapot. Then remove tea bags and add other ingredients.

Calories per serving: 114   Vitamin C: Excellent

SUN TEA

Preparation: 3–4 hours

Place 9 Red Rose Tea Bags in a 20-cup (5 L) glass jar and fill with cold water. Smaller families can use 2 tea bags in a 4-cup (1 L) jar. Cover and place outside in the hot sunshine for 3–4 hours. If the sun is less intense, increase the time accordingly. (Refrigerate within 5 hours from the start of brewing in intense sunlight.) Remove tea bags, squeezing gently. To serve, pour tea over ice in glasses. Sweeten with low-calorie sweetener or Simple Sugar Syrup (recipe follows); garnish with sliced orange lime or lemon, mint leaves or maraschino cherries.

TIP: Serve Sun Tea over fruit ice cubes made by freezing colorful fruit juices.

CYCLER'S SPECIAL

This tea is perfect for use at the cottage, campground and all outdoor lifestyle activities.

2 cups	Sun Tea	500 mL
4 cups	apple juice	1 L
1¼ cups	fruit punch	300 mL
2	lemons, sliced	2
	Simple Sugar Syrup (recipe follows) *or* low-calorie substitute (e.g. Equal)	

In a large pitcher, combine Sun Tea, apple juice, fruit punch and lemon slices. Sweeten to taste with Sugar Syrup or low-calorie sugar substitute. Serve with ice.

Makes fifteen ½-cup (125 mL) servings.

Simple Sugar Syrup: In a small saucepan, bring 1 cup (250 mL) sugar and 1 cup (250 mL) water to a boil until sugar has dissolved. Cool. Makes 1 cup (250 mL). For a change, pour hot syrup over chopped mint leaves, cool and strain.

Makes approximately 7 servings.

Calories per serving: 103   Vitamin C: Excellent

SUNSHINE COOLER

Preparation: about 5 minutes after tea is cool

Bound to be popular with "kids" from nine to ninety, this drink is a winning combination of three popular summer drinks — iced tea, ice-cream float and ice-cream soda.

½ cup	boiling water	125 mL
2	Red Rose Tea Bags	2
2 tbsp	white sugar	25 mL
1 cup	orange juice, chilled	250 mL
	club soda, chilled	
	Vanilla ice cream	

Pour boiling water over tea bags; brew 5 minutes; remove tea bags, stir in sugar and cool. To serve, combine tea with juice. Pour into glasses, top with splash of soda and scoop of ice cream.

Makes 2 servings.

Calories per serving: 128   Vitamin C: Excellent

TANGY ORANGE HEALTH SHAKE

Preparation: about 5 minutes after tea is cool

Wake up with this nutritious start to your morning or drink it throughout the day whenever you need a spur-of-the-moment nutrition break.

1 cup	boiling water	250 mL
2	Lipton Tangy Orange Herbal Tea Bags	2
1	banana	1
2/3 cup	plain yogurt	150 mL
1 tbsp	liquid honey	15 mL

Pour boiling water over herbal tea bags. Brew 5 minutes; remove tea bags, cool. In a blender or food processor, blend all ingredients at high speed until smooth and frothy.

Makes 2 cups (500 mL), about 2 servings.

TIP: Prepare the Herbal Tea the night before and refrigerate. Blend instantly for breakfast.

Calories per serving: 133

SURPRISE SHAKES

Herbal Tea is the surprise addition to these milkshakes. It adds a tantalizing taste to the smooth coolness of the shakes.
Try:
• Equal amounts of sweetened iced Citrus Sunset Herbal Tea and vanilla ice cream or rainbow sherbet.

• Equal amounts of sweetened iced Lemon Soother Herbal Tea and lemon sherbet.
• Equal amounts of sweetened Tangy Orange Herbal Tea and orange sherbet.

SPICY LEMONADE

Preparation: about 5 minutes after tea is cool

Make extra Herbal Tea when you're preparing this drink and use it to freeze into ice cubes. As they melt, they won't dilute the drink.

1 1/2 cups	boiling water	375 mL
3	Lipton Cinnamon Apple Herbal Tea Bags	3
1	can (12.5 fl. oz/355 mL) frozen lemonade, thawed	1
2 cups	cold water	500 mL

Combine herbal tea, lemonade and cold water. Serve over ice cubes.

Makes ten 1/2-cup (125 mL) servings.

TIPS: 1. Use 1 Lipton Herbal Tea Bag for each cup of boiling water when preparing ice cubes or ice ring. Choose compatible Herbal Tea flavor for ice cubes with the beverage being served. 2. Frosted glasses add a nice touch to iced Herbal Tea beverages. Simply dip the glass rim in fruit juice and then in sugar.

In a teapot, pour boiling water over herbal tea bags. Brew 5 minutes; remove tea bags, cool.

Calories per serving: 40

KIWIFRUIT DAIQUIRIS

Preparation: about 5 minutes

Kiwifruit is also known as the Chinese gooseberry. Fortunately, it doesn't have the pucker-power of gooseberries, but a taste resembling honeydew melon.

1	kiwifruit, pared and quartered	1
2–3 tsp	sugar	10–15 mL
1 tbsp	lime juice	15 mL
1–2 oz	rum (optional)	25–50 mL
1 drop	green food color (optional)	1
8	ice cubes, crushed	8
2	kiwifruit slices	2

In a blender or food processor, purée all ingredients except 2 kiwifruit slices until smooth. Pour into 2 stemmed glasses and garnish with sliced kiwifruit.

Makes 2 servings.

Calories per serving: 42   Vitamin C: Excellent

VARIATION

Strawberries, raspberries or banana may replace kiwifruit.

GLISTENING CHAMPAGNE PUNCH

Preparation: about 10 minutes

Special celebrations call for a special punch. This is it! To make it even more festive, use a decorated ice ring or float flowers on the surface of the punch bowl.

1½ cups	sugar	375 mL
2 cups	freshly squeezed lemon juice	500 mL
2	bottles (750 mL) dry white wine, chilled	2
1	bottle (750 mL) champagne, chilled	1
½ cup	brandy	125 mL
½ cup	orange-flavored liqueur (optional)	125 mL
1	lemon, thinly sliced	1
1½ cups	sliced strawberries, fresh or frozen	375 mL

Stir sugar into lemon juice until dissolved; chill thoroughly. Just before serving, pour over ice mold or ice ring in punch bowl. Gently stir in white wine and champagne; add brandy and orange-flavored liqueur, if desired. Garnish with lemon slices and sliced strawberries.

Makes approximately twenty-five ½-cup (125 mL) servings.

TIP: To make a clear ice mold or ring use club soda instead of water. If pieces of fruit are to be added to the mold, freeze a layer of soda until almost set, add fruit and freeze again. Add remaining club soda and freeze until firm.

Calories per serving: 160   Vitamin C: Excellent

SOBER SANGRIA

Preparation: about 5 minutes

This punch will be a show-stopper centerpiece at your party when you use a round watermelon shell as a punch bowl. Tuck green and variegated leaves around the base along with clusters of watermelon balls and green grapes.

1	can (6 fl. oz / 170 mL) frozen orange juice concentrate	1
2 cups	cranberry juice	500 mL
2 tbsp	lemon juice	25 mL
1 cup	diced fruit (e.g. apple, orange, lime or lemon)	250 mL
1	bottle (750 mL) chilled cream soda *or* club soda	1

Prepare orange juice according to can directions. In a large pitcher, combine orange, cranberry, lemon juice with fruit; refrigerate. At serving time, add cream soda.

Makes approximately sixteen ½-cup (125 mL) servings.

Calories per serving: 65   Vitamin C: Excellent

VARIATION

Not-So-Sober Sangria: Replace cranberry juice with dry red wine and cream soda with club soda.

TIP: Add sugar according to taste preference but don't make it too sweet. Authentic Sangria is full-bodied and fruity but not very sweet.

MEXICAN COFFEE

Preparation: about 10 minutes

A perfect ending for a Mexican meal is this fabulous dessert coffee.

¼ cup	unsweetened cocoa	50 mL
¾ cup	brown sugar	175 mL
2 tsp	cinnamon	10 mL
5 cups	coffee	1.25 L
	Tia Maria or Kahlua liqueur	
	Whipped cream	

In a large saucepan, combine cocoa, brown sugar, cinnamon and coffee. Heat until sugar dissolves and coffee is hot. Pour into cups, add liqueur and top with whipped cream. Or, liqueur may be served separately.

TIP: To save time use 5 tsp (25 mL) instant coffee granules and 5 cups (1.25 L) boiling water to replace brewed coffee.

Calories per serving: 137, without liqueur and whipped cream

INDEX